CHILCOTIN
YARNS

CHILCOTIN YARNS

Bruce Watt

H
HERITAGE

VICTORIA | VANCOUVER | CALGARY

Heritage House Publishing Company Ltd.
heritagehouse.ca

LIBRARY AND ARCHIVES CANADA CATALOGUING IN PUBLICATION

Watt, Bruce, 1926–
    Chilcotin yarns / Bruce Watt.

Issued also in electronic format.
ISBN 978-1-927051-43-6

    1. Watt, Bruce, 1926–. 2. Country life—British Columbia—Big Creek—Anecdotes.
3. Big Creek (B.C.)—Biography. I. Title.

Edited by Kate Scallion and Karla Decker
Proofread by Lesley Cameron
Cover and book design by Jacqui Thomas
Front cover: Roddy and Dee bucking up firewood courtesy of the author;
    wood by sayram/istockphoto.com; photo borders by 221A/istockphoto.com
Back cover: sketch by Jacqui Thomas
All interior photos courtesy of the author. Sketches by Jacqui Thomas based on original drawings
    by the author. Photo borders by belterz/iStockphoto.com and 221A/iStockphoto.com

MIX
Paper from
responsible sources
FSC FSC® C016245

The interior of this book was produced on 100% post-consumer recycled paper, processed chlorine free and printed with vegetable-based inks.

Heritage House acknowledges the financial support for its publishing program from the Government of Canada through the Canada Book Fund (CBF), Canada Council for the Arts and the province of British Columbia through the British Columbia Arts Council and the Book Publishing Tax Credit.

Canadian Patrimoine
Heritage canadien

The Canada Council | Le Conseil des Arts
for the Arts | du Canada

BRITISH COLUMBIA
ARTS COUNCIL

16 15 14 13 12 1 2 3 4 5

Printed in Canada

For my family

CONTENTS

SORT OF A PREFACE

Some of the yarns you are about to read may be Chilcotinized a very little bit. To Chilcotinize a story or experience, the storyteller may wander from the absolute truth. Some of the yarns that were told to me could possibly be not totally true. The teller of the yarn may not have good recall, or may have been attempting to make a better story. Chilcotinizing is accepted by any true Chilcotin.

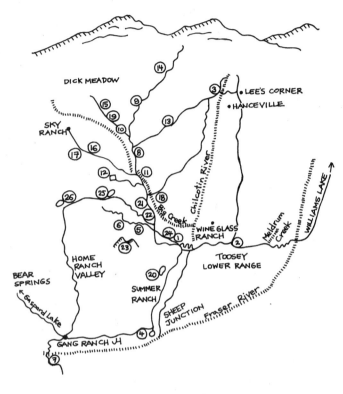

1	Farwell Place
2	Riske Creek
3	Chilco Ranch T2
4	Dry Farm (Spring Range)
5	Summer Range Creek
6	Gang Ranch Corrals
7	Gang Ranch Bridge
8	Big Creek P.O. ✕
9	Bell Ranch ᴍ ᴃ 7⁄
10	Bambrick Ranch ☲
11	Lightning Cattle Co. ⌄ (Home Place)
12	Paul St. Pierre's cabin on Square Lake
13	Veera Bonner's place on Fletcher Lake (Bin Go Shaw)

14	Duane Witte's Ranch ⋀ ♡
15	Henry Ranch
16	Mons Lake
17	Watt Meadow
18	Scallon Ranch
19	Frank Witte's Ranch $
20	Poison Lake
21	Sugarcane Jacks
22	Jameson Meadow
23	Saddle Horse Mountain
24	Gang Horse Pasture
25	Happy Ann Flat
26	Burnt Meadow

THE START

My wife, Phyllis, and I came into the Chilcotin on May 6, 1948. We had been married for about six weeks, and I was beginning a job working for her uncle, Dick Church, at the Big Creek Ranching Company. We came in with a hired three-ton truck. We had all the furniture we owned in the front end of the truck bed, including a piano that still bears the scars of that trip. In the back end we had two horses, one Phyllis had raised and one I had raised.

In those days you didn't drive that road from the Fraser Valley into the Chilcotin alone, especially in May. You travelled in a convoy of at least three vehicles so if someone got stuck, the other two could pull him out. There was a pretty good chance of getting stuck—in fact, it was inevitable.

The truck drivers we'd hired, who were from the coast, didn't believe they would need chains, shovels, axes or anything like that. However, Phyllis's mother, who was born and raised in this country, insisted that we take these things with us. We took everything with us except the chains.

When we arrived in Williams Lake, we met Dick Church and Neville Blenkinsop, another rancher in the Big Creek area, who were to join our convoy. When they found out that our truck drivers still thought they didn't need chains, Dick and Neville were adamant that we wouldn't get into Big Creek without them. In the end, we had to rustle around and get some, and it was good that we did.

We took off in the morning in the three trucks, and the road was all dirt (or mud). We arrived at Lee's Corner, about 60 miles from Williams Lake, after a few hours and the road just got rougher and rougher as we went along. We decided that it would be far better to ride the horses the last 21 miles into the ranch than have them bouncing around in the back of the truck. We unloaded the two horses and I struck off, starting out half an hour ahead of the trucks while Phyllis stayed with Dick and Neville.

I thought I'd never get there. I was leading one horse and riding the other, and I switched horses as I went along to spell them off. By the time I'd climbed up the hill from the Chilco Ranch I was already looking for Big Creek. I'd only gone a few miles, but it sure felt a lot longer. It was a long time before I got there. The road was so muddy you couldn't do anything but walk the horses, and not even a fast walk at that. The first hint of civilization I came upon was about a mile out of Big Creek. It was a sign that said SLOW TO 15 MPH. The sign was because of a little log schoolhouse there, and you really were supposed to slow down to go by it. But I don't think anyone ever even got up to 15 mph in that particular area! It was late, and my butt was sore when I finally arrived at the ranch. I'd thought those trucks would have passed me long ago, but I figured they were stuck. They were, of course. I beat them to the ranch by two hours, and I walked the horses nearly all the way. Neville Blenkinsop's truck never did make it. The transmission got torn out at a place called Indian Meadow.

We received a great welcome to the place. We put the horses away, then were taken over and shown the little log cabin that was to be our home. Knowing we were newlyweds, the Church family had gone to a great deal of trouble to fix the place up. They'd even hand-planed the cabin floor. Now that is quite a contract; they did saw their own lumber on the ranch, but a planed floor was really rare—even a floor was not too common. Prior to our coming, it had been a dirt floor.

Dick's wife, Rona, and Queenie, Gerald Blenkinsop's wife, had argued about this cabin floor. Rona, who was originally from a soft life in Victoria, thought we should have the luxury of a floor, but Queenie felt we should start out rough, as most homesteaders did— no floor at all, let alone a planed one. I tell you, it did look nice, this white Jack-pine planed floor in our small cabin. It was where we were to spend the next two years of our life. We got settled in and then were ready to go to work.

The deal I had was that we received $80 a month, plus beef, milk and eggs whenever the weather and dogs would allow. If we beat the dogs to the eggs, then we got them. As it turned out, having beef was an uncommon occurrence. In two years, we probably only had beef twice. The rest of the meat was deer and moose, because there was no refrigeration except in the winter. We managed to put away $56 of the $80 in the bank every month over the next two years. We lived on the balance, and we lived pretty well. We didn't go dining and dancing very much, but we really had a good life.

Not many of the holes in the meadows were as easy to spot as this one, or it would have been a lot more boring out there chasing horses.

HUNTING HORSES
AND DODGING JACK PINES

One of the first jobs I had was to hunt horses at a place called Dick Meadow. We were after horses that had been turned out to pasture and wandered off. The ranch foreman, Jim Bonner, and I packed a lunch and took off. There was no trucking or trailering of horses; the roads made it impossible. To hunt horses at Dick's in those days, you rode.

The first thing you had to do was ride 25 miles to the range, and from there you started hunting the horses. Well, mainly you hunted tracks. Neither Dick nor Jim believed in using bells on the horses too much. Instead, they would hunt for tracks until they found the freshest ones from the horses they wanted. Then they would track down these horses. Sometimes this would entail another 20 miles of riding, and then you still had to get back to the ranch.

I was riding the gelding I had brought up from the coast. That was one thing I did right, bringing along a good horse. He was a big, stout horse who could stand a lot of riding, and he had enough Arab in him that he was tough. However, I brought a saddle that wasn't quite so shiny. It was what in those days was called an "ass-buster," and it was. By the time I got back from that first ride, I couldn't even swing my leg over the saddle. I had to kind of ease out over the back end and then just crumple onto the ground. However, being young, I straightened out pretty quick and we put in many rides like that over the next two or three years.

I got so I really enjoyed chasing horses up in that country. The area itself was pretty western, and you couldn't find anywhere more rugged to run horses. All over the meadows are large holes, like big bomb craters lined with rocks, with swamp grass growing right up to the edge. Sometimes when you were running, you wouldn't see them until you were right on top of them. Of course, your horse wouldn't either. It would jump one of those and you would think you were all straightened out, but then you would run into another one. That has got to be one of the worst pieces of country that I ever chased horses in, but I grew to love the challenge. At least out on the meadows you didn't have to jump or duck trees. You got off that meadow, away from the craters, and you'd think you had it made, but then you'd be right into the trees. That was something else again. I found ducking Jack pines scared me for a while, and I never managed to enjoy it much.

What I found about chasing horses in the Jack pines was that I only had trouble until I hit the first tree. This generally made me so mad that from then on, it didn't bother me a darn bit. After the first tree I smacked with my knee, I was away. I knew I could run horses all day.

Some days we could travel forever without finding any fresh grass on the range. It got easier once the snow melted.

SPRING TURNOUT
AND WINTERING OUT

As we settled into ranch life at Big Creek, one of the first things Phyllis had to learn was how to cook. She had been raised on a ranch in Abbotsford, and they had a lot of sheep and chickens. I found out later she never did any cooking because she was going to school. I was a little suspicious when we opened our wedding present from her older brother, Richard. It was a kettle that whistled when the water boiled, and he said he was afraid she knew so little about cooking that she wouldn't even know how to boil water. Luckily, she knew how to bake bread.

I can remember coming in for lunch one day when Phyllis had been trying to cook pies. She had never cooked a pie before, and to top it off, she was using a wood stove that didn't have any regulators or gauges on it; it was just an old-time cookstove. As I was coming across the yard—fortunately, I wasn't too close to the house—I saw these two pies come flying right out the front door. Out into the yard they came, and did they bounce!

She did pass the supreme test in cooking ability later, having learned to cook moose meat in such a way that the old cow men thought they were eating beef. She didn't get a lot of time to learn about cooking in the first three years we were married, though, because she worked outside with me whenever there was an opportunity.

If there was any cowboying to do in the way of chasing cattle, Phyllis would go along every trip, though she never did take to chasing horses. She had to do it every once in a while, but she didn't like those Jack pines too well, so she restricted her cowboying to working with the cattle.

She did a lot of riding with me; we would take jobs during the spring and summer looking after the cattle for the Big Creek Stockmen's Association. We'd go down with the cattle onto the lower turnouts and stay for six weeks in one area. There would be just the two of us watching over the cattle, looking for any problems such as bears or sickness, in which case we would also do the doctoring. We had about six or seven horses that we used. It was very steep terrain on the Chilcotin River, and it was hard on the horses. We had to have enough horses so we could spell them off every other day. After six weeks, we would move the cattle up into what we called the Upper Big Creek Turnout, and then we would move our camp up there too. Life was very good on the range. We lived in a Chilcotin-style wall tent, generally built with logs four feet high, and then the tent went on top of the last round of logs. We made a bed out of fir boughs. Once you learned how to make one of these beds, it was just about as good a bed as you could sleep on. We also had a little stove in the tent, which was always positioned so we could just reach out in the morning and start it without getting out of bed. When we went down to the river country in late March, the mornings were still pretty cold; that heat felt really good when you first got out of bed. We had to pack our water a little ways—about a quarter of a mile—to the camp, but we had lots of horse feed down there. There was no end of deer all around us, and lots of ducks too. Once the ducks came in, we had plenty of fresh meat.

We would often go six weeks to two months without seeing another living soul, and that was just fine. In fact, it was really good. The work wasn't hard. Most days, you just had to ride out and check the cattle. It was pretty good going for a young couple.

In the winter we would often take a job feeding cattle up in the mountains, which were only 12 to 14 miles from the ranch. Once again, we'd go back up there and live in an old cabin. When we first went into one place, a cabin that belonged to Cecil Henry, a neighbouring rancher, we were feeding cattle at the S and Dolly Meadows, two areas that belonged to Dick Church.

At that time the cattle were rustling out and all we were feeding were pellets. A cow rustles with its nose and a horse rustles by pawing the snow to get at the grass underneath. If it warmed up in the winter and then froze, a crust would form on the snow that sometimes would be bad enough to make rustling very hard for cows, as their noses would get sore. One solution was to turn a bunch of horses in with the cows. They would paw the snow and the cows would steal the grass they had uncovered. The pellets were a supplement food to go along with the grass.

There was good rustling in that country, so we would get up early in the morning, ride out and feed the pellets to the herd. We would be pretty well done by 10:30 or 11:00 AM, and we only had to ride a total of 14 miles maybe. It wasn't a hard day, except it could be 30 degrees below zero.

Our cabin was not a good one. And because it would get so cold at night, we had to pour all the water out of the kettles and buckets or they would freeze and break. All we had to sit on were a couple of blocks of wood. That can get quite uncomfortable if you are sitting around in the evening and you want to read, so I decided to make some easy chairs. I cut some small Jack pines and made two frames, one for Phyllis and one for me, but we had to have something to cover these chairs. At the time there were a lot of moose around; it was nothing to count 30 moose in any one of the meadows. We didn't give a second thought to shooting moose for just about anything we needed, and in this case we needed a hide to cover those two chairs.

The gun I packed in those days was an old Ranger 30-30. These guns were very common then; after the war, you could buy one for about five dollars. I liked to shoot, but I had to do quite a bit of practising with this 30-30 as it was quite different from the .22 I had done most of my shooting with. I had used up most of our shells trying to get the 30-30 sighted in the way I wanted it. I had taken the conventional sight off and put a peep sight on; trying to get this lined up used most of our limited supply of shells.

However, one morning we went out and I saw a cow moose across the meadow, so I shot it. I walked across the meadow thinking I'd just cut its throat to finish it off and then skin it. Instead, the moose stood up and came after me. I had left my horse with Phyllis and was walking in the snow wearing full-length leather chaps, which made it hard to get away from the moose. Fortunately, there was a tree right handy to where it started chasing me. I couldn't climb the tree, but I kept going around it and I got one more shot—my final one—into the moose. But this never slowed the beast down, and we went around and around this tree. It was all in slow motion—at least it seemed that way to me (my motions, that is, not the moose's).

Phyllis thought all this was pretty funny, and she was just standing there watching that moose chase me around and around that tree! Finally it died from its wounds, and I was able to skin it.

By the time we got the hide back to our camp, it was getting quite dark. As I was stretching the hide over the chairs, I wasn't being too careful about what I was doing, but I did get the two chairs put together. As I sat down in the chair I had rigged for myself, I leaned my head back and it felt kind of clammy right on the back of my neck. It was comfortable, except for that. Then I realized I had put the cow moose's udder right where my head reached. I had to remodel the chair, cutting this area out.

You would have thought that the hide would dry up and damage the frames, but the chairs were stout and the drying didn't hurt the frames at all. Those chairs lasted in that cabin for 15 years and were quite comfortable.

Another winter when we got into the mountain meadows, there had been a thaw and then a freeze-up, and we didn't have any ice shoes to put on the horses; their hooves were just slick. You can get away with that pretty good when there is just snow on the ground, but when that ice comes, it gets a little hairy. I will never forget how much Phyllis hated to ride on that ice because the horse was slipping and sliding around. When we had to go down and get the mail and some groceries and we rode down on that ice, I'll tell you, it was a pretty scary trip.

STRESS

Ranching has never been a very lucrative business, and most people go into it for the lifestyle. This more than offset the lack of financial gain. Some say that if you have one good year in 40, you are doing well.

Subsidizing your lack of income was something nearly everyone in the business practised. Guiding was one way to subsidize, and most of us did this. There was lots of game in those days and not as many endangered species. You had to guide under a licensed guide for a few years until you could get your licence and be allotted a territory to guide in. Fortunately, I got to guide for three of the best: Duane Witte, Cecil Henry and Dick Church.

Dick was the first guide I started with, and he was noted as the best in the business. On our first trip, we packed two days back into what they called the Snow Mountains. We were after sheep and grizzlies.

After setting up camp, we placed bear bait in an opening we could see from the trail we used every day on our way up to the timberline; it was in good hunting territory. Today you are not allowed to bait bear of some species because they have become endangered.

My hunting experience at this point was zilch, so Dick would just point me at some mountain and I would strike off for the day with my hunters. Fortunately, I was always riding an old hunting horse that really knew the country and, of course, had the ability all horses have, when you give them their head to take you right back to camp.

About halfway through the day, I'd give my horse its head and soon we would be heading straight for camp. Of course, sometimes the hunters would shoot something and by the time they'd dressed it out, it would be dark. Finding our way back to camp in the dark might sound kind of tough, but it isn't for a horse. We'd be travelling along in the pitch dark and I would have no idea where we were when, much to my surprise, there was our campfire. The hunters told Dick how I brought them home in the dark and hit camp right on the button. Amazing! Yeah, well . . .

On one of our hunts, Cecil Henry was guiding with us. We were on our way out one morning and noticed that our bait was completely gone. This bait weighed about 1,400 pounds. A grizzly was the only animal capable of dragging that much weight. The bait had been in an opening that was half-surrounded on the bottom side by a burn that had reseeded itself with second growth that was so thick you could not ride through it. This is where the bear had taken the bait. We developed a plan whereby I was to stay with the hunters on the edge of the opening, and Cecil and Dick would track the bear and maybe get it to go across the opening where the hunters could get a crack at it.

Dick and Cecil picked up the bear's track at the bait, which wasn't far into the burn, and started tracking it. They tied up their horses at the edge of the burn, as it was too thick with trees to ride through. Dick was in the lead, doing the tracking, and Cecil was right behind. Dick had his rifle over his shoulder, packing it by the barrel. His rifle was a .250-3000 with a four-power scope. This weapon is not much better than a cork gun against grizzlies, but it was the gun Dick had used when he shot a grizzly that held the record for widest skull for many years.

Then Dick and Cecil came to a place where they could see their own tracks following the bear's—and its tracks now with theirs. This meant the bear could now be behind them, following them.

These were two of the toughest men I have ever known, but I think what is nowadays referred to as stress was starting to sneak up on them. Dick was leading, his rifle held barrel head down, being as quiet as possible, with Cecil right behind him. Cecil had to blow his nose—maybe because of nervous tension—so he put his finger on one nostril and blew hard. He opened his eyes quickly and found himself looking right down the barrel of a .250-3000.

That was pretty well the end of the hunt that day.

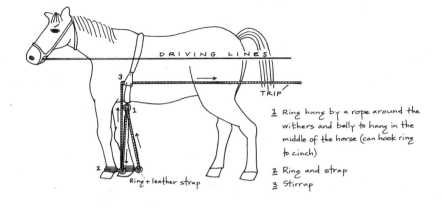

DRIVING LINES

TRIP

1 Ring hung by a rope around the withers and belly to hang in the middle of the horse (can hook ring to cinch)

2 Ring and strap

3 Stirrup

Ring + leather strap

ROUGH HORSES

We had been at Dick's for a little over a year when he decided to break some horses that he had brought in from Alberta. He contracted an old horse breaker from the nearby Stone Reserve, Benny Stobie, to do the job.

Benny rode for the Frontier Cattle Company in his younger days, and he was one tough hand. Frontier was the company made famous by *Grass Beyond the Mountains* and probably the first ranch in the Chilcotin to have workers' compensation. Once, apparently, the crew ran out of cups on a roundup, so Benny took to drinking his coffee out of a rusty tin can. Well, he soon went blind—not totally blind, but close. As a result, Benny received compensation for the rest of his life. I'm not sure whether it was the can or what he was drinking out of it that was the problem.

Anyway, Dick gave me the job of assisting Benny. Benny got 15 dollars per head, and we were supposed to be able to ride the horses outside the big corral in three days. The youngest horses were 8 years old, and the oldest were 12. These horses were all range-raised and had not even been halter-broke. I had grown up around horses, but the horses I had previously trained were halter-broke as weanlings, had been handled a lot and were ready to ride by the time they were two years old. What we were about to take on was totally removed from any experience I'd had.

So here we began: a blind guy and a green pea.

Every ranch in those days had a set of corrals. In nearly every case, there was a small corral about 11 good logs high that was gated into a bigger corral, about six times larger. The plan was to get the horses to a point where we could ride them in the small corral and then ease them out into the big one. From there, we'd open the gate of the big corral, and then we were on our own outside.

First we would cut the horse that we were going to work on from the group and get it into the small corral. Then we would rope its two front feet, get behind it and stay behind it while pulling on the rope until the horse went down. It was important to stay as directly behind the horse as possible, as that way it would go down quicker and easier. Once the horse was on the ground, we would keep its roped feet as high as we could so it could not struggle its way back up again. Nine times out of 10, in its kicking and struggling the horse would kick one hind leg between its roped front feet. You could then put a couple of half hitches on its three roped legs, and then the horse was hog-tied and down.

The next step, after we'd caught our breath, was to put a halter on. With one guy holding the horse's head down, it wasn't too hard to get a halter on. The halters we used in those days were made of heavy, soft rawhide. Once the halter was on, we'd put on the shank. This was a stout sisal rope, as there was no nylon on the scene yet. We would run the shank through the bottom of the noseband, back to the throatlatch, around it with one curl around the halter and back under the jaw, leaving enough slack to tie a bowline knot. Then, with some slack, we'd put a half hitch around the ring of the halter up front. This way, any violent pulling or jerking was on the rope and not the halter. We would always leave lots of shank for what came next.

Once the horse was up and had finished stampeding around the corral, the halter-breaking was next. This was the worst possible way of halter-breaking, but it was the only way we knew at the time. We would pull the horse off balance until it took a step towards us. Once it stepped forward, we would ease up and stroke its neck as a reward. It didn't take long before most horses would take several steps forward, and they were on their way to being halter-broke. This was a lot of work, and in later years we learned much easier ways of getting this job done.

Once the horse had stopped fighting the rope, we would tie it to the corral. We would leave it alone for a while to figure this out.

Sometimes it would bang its head a bit and maybe skin it up a little. In later years we came up with a much better way of letting the horse adjust to being tied up.

Next on the list was hobbling the horse. Benny used what is called the Wyoming hobble. The hobble material was about 16 feet of soft cotton rope that had a spliced eye on one end with the other end spliced back into the rope. One fellow (me) would hold the horse, and the other (Benny) would stand close to the horse's left shoulder, flicking the rope around the horse's front feet until the feel of the rope didn't bother the horse too much. Once the horse was used to that, Benny would flip the end of the rope with the eye in it so that it went around the horse's right front leg, from back to front. Then he picked up the rope with a wire that had a hook on one end, and pulled the looped end up towards where we were standing. Once that was sorted out, we'd let the horse get used to the feel of the rope on its legs.

Holding the looped end of the rope in his right hand and the loose end in the left hand, Benny's next step was to make two loops around the rope in his right hand. Then, taking the loop in front of the left leg, Benny would stick the spliced-back end through the loop and pull it snug. In effect, both front legs were roped with a double twist in the loop.

If you can follow this, you are very good.

Now, with both of the horse's front feet roped, we didn't give the horse any slack. If you kept the rope tight, the horse couldn't get out of it, and we would have some control over the animal. Next we would pick up the left hind leg by flipping the spliced-eye end of the rope between the hind legs in such a manner that we could hook the spliced end up to us. Now we could pick up the hind leg until the horse would quit kicking, leaving enough slack so that we would be holding the leg to the point where the horse could kick but the rope wouldn't burn its leg. The best way was to hold both looped pieces in one hand so if the horse did kick (and it did), we could give it slack without burning its leg.

Then, when the horse would lift its leg, we would pull the rope about 18 inches from the front legs. It is necessary to keep this distance because, with this hobble, the horse will probably go down, but with this allowance it can, and will, get up. Once we'd helped the horse put its foot down in position, we would then twist the spliced end around the loop and tie it to the front left leg. We would try to keep the rope above the ankles on both front legs and one hind leg. Once they have tried to escape this hobble a few times, most horses will figure it is just as well to stay put.

Now the horse is ready to sack out. The object of sacking out is to get the horse used to all of the things that would be used when riding it, and to try not to scare the hell out of it while doing it. We began by pulling the mane and tail, grooming the horse all over. We would first introduce it to saddle blankets and chaps, giving them some time to get used to each, and then we added pack canvases and oilskin coats. After a bit of this, it was time to saddle up. We would do this several times, getting on and off both sides. Then we would tie the hobble in such a manner that it could be jerked completely loose from the ground, or by the rider. The minute the hobble dropped would be the moment of truth, when the horse would quickly realize it was free.

Benny could get on a lot of these horses and not have much trouble. He had plenty of experience and the ability to ride if they tied one on or took off, and although he couldn't see very well, he had no fear.

Things were not that good for me—I had none of Benny's attributes. When the horse started bucking me, I would immediately start scouting out a place to land. They say when you start looking for a place to settle, you are already bucked off. Amen!

Some days you might not feel like you got much done, but you never felt like you had wasted any time just enjoying the beauty of this country.

WORK FOR NOTHING

Dick Church was taking Dave Stuart, a hunter from North Dakota, down to the lower country near Summer Range Creek and Poison Lake to hunt bear. I knew Dave, as I had been on a hunt with him and Dick the previous fall. Dave pretty well hunted all year round, and he was, bar none, the best shot we had ever seen. He could hit a running coyote at 300 yards. If he could see where his shots were landing for about two shots, the third shot would be lights out for the coyote. Dave's favourite gun was a wildcat gun: a .270 Magnum chambered to take a .300 Magnum case, necked down to the .270 bullet. Dave was a great hunter to guide. He was a good rider, excellent around camp and very down to earth. Tough going did not bother him at all, which was good, as he had hunted many times with Dick, and that meant you had to be tough to come back for more.

I knew they were coming by our place on their way down to Summer Range Creek and would stop in for tea and a visit. I got up and on the trail about daylight and rode two miles back towards Church's. I stayed in the timber all the way for two miles, never touching the road at all.

I tied up my horse not far from the road and walked to it. I broke off a small branch and stuck it in my back pocket. Then I proceeded to make bear tracks across the road. You can make a decent-looking bear track by folding your fist, keeping your thumb under your fingers and rolling your fist in the dust or mud. This makes a black bear track, which is what Dave and Dick were after. I made a pretty fair set of tracks across the road and then used the branch to wipe out my tracks as I backed away. Later in the morning, Dave and Dick tied up out by the front gate and came up to the house. We visited for a while, and not one word was said about the tracks. I couldn't believe Dick had missed the track: I had seen him spot a lynx track while driving a three-ton truck, and he even got the truck stopped before we ran over the track. This bugged me a bit, especially after all the trouble I had gone to. Getting Dave to one side a little later, I asked if Dick had seen any tracks on the way to our place.

"Well, there was a place about two miles back," Dave recalled. "I was riding alongside Dick, and he looked down and snorted a little [Dick did snort a bit, but not loud]. He said, 'Bruce has been out here fooling around.' And he just kept on riding, not even breaking stride."

I never bothered trying to fool Dick again.

Our place might not have looked quite so picturesque when Brian arrived, but after running 12 miles in gumboots, I'm sure it still looked pretty darn good!

CITY BOY

We hadn't been in the Chilcotin country very long when a friend of Phyllis's, Brian Bell-Irving, came up to visit us. He had quite an experience. It was 1948, and Brian had a brand-new Ford. It was a really fancy little car that he had just bought, and he came up the road from the Chilco Ranch, which was a sorry sort of a road in those days.

As Brian was driving in, he came upon two fellows who were walking down the road. They had just been fired by the Chilco Ranch and were put out at the country and everyone in it. So when he asked them the way in, they told him there was only one road in, and it was pretty good. They also misdirected poor Brian. They told him that when he came to Indian Meadow, which was a major nightmare for anyone driving there because it

35

was a big swamp, he would see kind of a mudhole. They told him that the secret was to build up a bunch of speed, hit it hard and he'd go right through.

Well, Brian was a city boy, and he certainly wasn't a tracker or he'd have noticed the route going around the mudhole. The mudhole was right in the middle of the road, so it did look like the road went in and out the other side. However, there were some tracks around it, which was how people were getting by it.

But these boys had said to back up the hill just before the mudhole to get a good run at 'er. So when Brian got there, he wound up his brand-new Ford pretty good and hit that mudhole hard. He did want to get in there to visit, after all.

He got about halfway across with his momentum. Fortunately, he got the window down and got out before his car went just about out of sight. Then he had to start walking. It was a 12-mile walk in a pair of gumboots.

This guy was a real athlete, a great rugby player and boxer, and he was a hell of a guy. He was born and raised in Vancouver, and he had never really been out in the bush before. That particular night Brian came in, the coyotes were howling, and naturally he didn't know the difference between a coyote howl and a wolf howl. He thought they were wolves, so he did a fast jog most of the way in. That was tough jogging, too, because there were ruts, and it was muddy and slippery. Fortunately, he was in pretty good shape when he started out.

It took a tractor, a three-ton truck, a bunch of pulleys and cables, a buried dead-man anchor and everything else we had to get that car out of there. Brian never did come back to visit, and I don't altogether blame him.

CALVING THE HEIFER

Calving out a bunch of heifers is not high on the list of things anyone likes doing on a ranch. Dick Church kept his heifers that were due to calve in a small pasture between two houses. One house belonged to Dick and his wife, Rona. Jim and Veera Bonner, Dick's foreman and his wife, lived in the other house. It was easy to keep an eye on the heifers during the day, and at night they had a rotation system to make sure that someone checked them out every two hours until daylight.

Dick Church had his own ideas on calving out his heifers. First, he did not want to disturb them once they started calving, and he didn't go near them unless they seemed to need help. Not a bad plan.

One day Jack Casselman and I were walking towards the heifer pasture and we saw Dick belly-crawling up to a heifer that was obviously having trouble. We hung back and watched; that seemed to be the best plan at the time.

Dick had managed to crawl up to the heifer's back end without her being aware of him because, of course, she was in distress. One method of helping a heifer is to slip a loop over one of her calf's feet and sit on the ground with your feet towards the front of the heifer, handy to her hams above the hocks. Then you take the other end of the rope—a piece of sash cord—behind your back and loop the other end to the calf's other foot. By putting a foot on each ham above the hock, straightening your legs and using your back, you can exert enough pressure to help the heifer get the calf out.

This was not a good day for Dick. He had just got into the right position to help when the heifer rolled her head up and spotted him. The wreck was on! She jumped up and took off running. The rope had slid up under Dick's armpits, and he was latched on. Fortunately, there were a lot of hummocks in this field, and they kept Dick airborne most of the trip; he'd just hit the top of these mounds every so often.

One side of the pasture was bordered by what is called a geographic boundary—Big Creek—and this young cow was heading straight for the river. Dick was flying much of the time, and there wasn't a sound from him. I figured he could have been knocked out, or maybe it was just another day on the ranch for him. He wasn't a big talker anyway.

Then, just as the heifer took to the air to land in the river, Dick hit a hummock with some willow bushes on top of it. This brought him to a sudden halt so abrupt that the calf popped out of the heifer and Dick didn't even get wet.

Now we had the heifer on the other side of the river and the calf on our side. When Dick got up he was wobbling a bit, but not too bad. He didn't say a whole lot, just headed for the house, as did we. The heifer, when she saw we'd all gone, came back across the river and mothered up with her calf.

Dick, I'm sure, figured that this was a successful operation, although I wouldn't recommend it. There are better ways.

I think Dick and I might have been as skinny as this young horse after we'd spent a week searching for some other horses that wandered off.

YOUNG HORSES

One of the better horse hunts I was ever on started one day late in spring. Dick told Jim Bonner and me to go up to the horse range and bring down a bunch of his young horses. These horses hadn't been seen for over a year, and we figured they may have wandered off the regular range.

Jim and I got an early start. We rode the 25 miles to the range and then started looking for some smaller tracks that these young horses would have left. Jim knew the country well, but we covered most of it without any luck. It was a little—what do they call it?—irksome to have to go back to the ranch and say we couldn't find them, but we had no choice.

"That's all right," said Rona, Dick's wife. "Dick will be back tomorrow, and he'll get them."

This was somewhat more irksome, but we knew she was right most of the time.

Well, Dick got home, told me to make a lunch to bring with us and we would go have another look the next day. The young ones had left the home range, but we covered that first just to make sure. We ate all of our lunch, which turned out to be a poor decision. That night we wound up at the Upper Hutch cabin and had to find something to eat. We did get lucky, as someone had left a little food in one of the cupboards. We found a soup-can-sized tin about two-thirds full of dehydrated onions. Then things got better: we found half a box of Rice Krispies. Both of these goods were dry, so it wasn't that difficult to pick out the signs of mice. We boiled the dehydrated onions and poured them over the Rice Krispies. Was it ever good! It was the best meal we'd had for a while.

Over the next four days we covered a lot of territory, but we couldn't find any sign of the horses. On the fifth night, we wound up at the Dick Meadow cabin, and I started hunting again for something to eat. Dick could do without eating, and he did just that many times. But he did smoke roll-your-own cigarettes right down to an eighth of an inch. One time a young fellow came to the ranch and offered Dick his first filter-tipped cigarette. We watched as he smoked it down halfway through the filter. Finally, the kid couldn't stand it and said to Dick, "Mr. Church, you are not supposed to smoke them down into the filter."

"Well, it never got any good till I got down there," replied Dick.

Fortunately, we found food in the Dick Meadow cabin. There was a little bit of flour and an old frying pan. We mixed the flour with some water, put it into the frying pan and put it over the fire. It went like concrete, and we had to scrape it out with our knives. After barely eating for the past few days, it sure tasted good. I may have tasted something as good since, but no better.

In the morning, Dick was looking over at some mountains that looked a hundred miles away and said, "You know, we haven't looked at the other side of that mountain. They may have drifted over there." I was kind of hoping he was kidding, but knew he wasn't. He wasn't much for kidding around.

We saddled up early and headed for the mountains. It wasn't a hundred miles, but we still didn't get there till noon. We had gone over the mountain and started down the other side when Dick said, "Here we are. They were here this spring after that wet snow." He struck off, trailing these horses down the mountain, and I was straining my eyeballs to see a track but saw nothing. Then we came upon some manure. I could see that, but nothing else. It was a long way between droppings sometimes, but Dick was going along as if there was a yellow line to follow.

Finally I pulled my horse up and asked, "What are you looking at to follow, and how do you know they were here after the wet snow?" Dick was a very good teacher and never did BS me. I don't think he did, anyway.

"Do you remember in the spring after everything had bared off and we got one more shot of winter with a couple of inches of wet snow?" Dick asked. "This kind of snow will ball up a bit on a horse's feet, and in those balls will be some grass that gets picked up. When the balls get knocked off, or just fall off, the balls will melt and leave those little curvatures of grass you can see easily," he explained.

Well, not that easily, but I could see them with some heavy looking.

We came upon the horses about an hour later and headed them for the top end of Groundhog Creek. They handled easily, and we took them along the creek and corralled them at Cecil Henry's camp farther down the creek.

We spent the night with Cecil and his kids, and ate quite a feast. The next day was an easy 35 miles home. We had been gone for seven days, and nobody was worried.

From then on, I never ventured very far without at least a bunch of those big Milk-Bone dog biscuits with my gear. They're light, and I've heard they're good for your teeth, too.

LET THERE BE LIGHT

The night was black as black one evening when we were going to a dance at the Big Creek Hall in our democrat wagon. Knowing that we would be travelling in total darkness, I decided to make a light for the democrat.

We used to get our white gas and kerosene in almost square four-gallon cans. I wired a small pole up the front and to one side of the democrat, cut the front out of one of these gas cans and wired a gas lamp inside it. Then I wired the can to the top end of the pole. There you are—a good headlight, if only a tad haywire.

We hooked up the team to go. One of the pair, Monty, was considered pretty well bombproof. The other horse was Cisco, and he wasn't so bombproof.

At the time we only had two kids. When we loaded up to go, we put one child on the floor of the democrat, and Phyllis held the other in her arms. I lit the lamp inside the can, and away we went. We felt pretty uptown with that light. It lit up the team and some of the trail. All was good.

The road was anything but smooth, and the can and lamp were doing some jiggling, which eventually jiggled one mantle off the light. Flames started coming around one side of the can.

"I think that outfit could explode," exclaimed Phyllis.

Now, I was sure someone in a physics class I'd once attended said that if gas is burning as fast as it leaks, the container won't explode.

So, I said, "It can't explode. And see all the light it's giving now! You can see the whole trail."

It was right about that moment that the other mantle gave up, and we had an even brighter light, as flames were coming out both sides of the can. You could see the whole countryside.

The team of horses was getting a little antsy for some reason—maybe because the flames were coming back over Phyllis's head and she had to lean forward some to avoid them. Phyllis was a bit more nervous by now too, and she said again, "I think this outfit could explode!"

"There is no way it will explode," I reassured her. I'd no sooner said the word "explode" when KABOOM! There was a fair explosion and a huge light, and you could see two horses going straight into orbit. The explosion was so big, it straightened out the gas can so it looked like a long silver flag on the pole.

We had been running a little late for the dance, but by the time I got the team settled down after they took off, we were early for the dance. Some good comes out of most experiences.

We ended up dancing until well after dawn, so it was daylight when we were making our way home again. We found the lamp on our way back. With a big hole blown out of one side, it didn't look repairable—and even if you could repair it, you couldn't trust it after the way it had acted.

We may have found the lamp, but I did lose something that night. Ever since, whenever I would make a positive statement such as "We can't get stuck in that mudhole!" I'd hear "There is no way it can explode."

(Note: I believe I failed physics.)

THE FLYING DUTCHMAN

John Siebert and I were heading for the Poison Lake country one time to hunt for some cows. We also had with us a young fellow from Holland. This young fellow connected with us through some shirt-tailed relative of ours from back east and stayed with us for a summer. We wouldn't have called him a "dude," as everyone has to start their knowledge somewhere and his was starting here. He was a very nice young guy and had taken English in school, so he could sort of understand what we were saying. We, in our wisdom and originality, had nicknamed him Dutchie.

Dutchie's knowledge of cowboys and riding had been learned from reading many cowboy magazines and funny papers. He did have a fair knowledge of the Lone Ranger and Tonto.

We had been riding a couple of hours and had just crossed Summer Range Creek, not far from Poison Lake, when we saw a Bennett wagon in the distance, coming our way. John always spoke low and slow, and you would have to believe he was very serious.

John stopped his horse and said, "Oh-oh, Indians!"

Dutchie pulled his horse up and asked, "They are all right, aren't they?"

"You never know," replied John.

Of course, we had recognized our good friend Phillip Myers and his family from the Stone Reserve in the wagon. They were just travelling from one part of the country to another, fishing and hunting as they went. They were just poking along in no hurry, and when somehow one of the lines to the bit got under the tongue of the wagon. Phillip stopped the team and got off to straighten things out.

"Oh-oh, they are getting ready to attack," said John.

I sidled over a little so I could see how Dutchie was taking all of this. He was already gone. I looked around and got a good view of the dust trail he was leaving as he headed back for Holland. Fortunately, we had given him a slow horse, so we turned him back before he made it.

By this time, Phillip had turned off the trail to go on down to the Gang Ranch corrals and cabin on Summer Range Creek. The dust settled, and we went on the trail again, heading for Poison Lake without Phillip and his family in sight.

John waited a bit as we rode along a ways and then said, "Now, that was lucky."

COLD RIDING

Corrals meant for holding wild horses were generally built where there was a known horse trail either going to or near a fair stand of Jack pines. The corrals were high and strong, generally just Jack-pine rails wired up to trees in a circle, with a gate that was fairly easy to shut or shift. Long "wings" fanned out from the gate to help funnel the horses into the corral. Of course, the longer the wings, the better. They could be three or four rails high, with the top rail just high enough that a running horse wouldn't try to jump it and the lowest rail low enough that colts wouldn't try to skim under it. To lengthen these wings, we would sometimes take a roll of cheesecloth, which was cheap enough in those days, hook the end of a roll on to the end of the wing, and roll it out about four feet off the ground through the trees. As a rule, this was enough to turn the horses down the funnel. The cloth is white and foreign to the horses, and they shy away from it and rarely try to run through it. I never saw a horse test this wing addition.

One winter the Gang Ranch decided to run in some of the wild horses from the Burnt Meadow country, and they built one of these wild-horse corrals on a trail frequently used by the horses.

I was one of 14 cowboys involved in this effort, and we were all staying in the cabin at Summer Range Creek. The furniture in the cabin consisted of a pot-bellied stove, a small table and two Coleman stoves that we cooked on. There wasn't room for anything more; when you get 14 men sleeping on the floor, that's about it for space. Most of us had pretty good bedrolls, and the ones who didn't were the ones who got up in the night to stoke the fire.

We were there a few days building the corral and wings, and when these were done, we started executing a rather elaborate plan to get the horses in. The plan was to split up into pairs and head in the direction of Burnt Meadow and Happy Ann Flat. Modern times had kicked in by this time and we had the use of a small airplane. I was chosen to be the spotter, as I had hunted horses for several years and was most familiar with the area.

We were searching in an area just a shade off the perimeter of the Gang Ranch, and within some of the range around our ranch. We would have left the wild herd alone, except that it was cutting good mares out of our domestic herd of horses. To get them back was difficult and we were not always successful.

My role in our plan was to spot a herd from the airplane and, by circling it, we would signal its location to the cowboys on the ground. They would then converge on the wild horses from different directions and run them in. Sounds simple enough, but it wasn't exactly.

We allowed the cowboys about an hour and a half to get to the area around Burnt Meadow. From the air, I soon spotted a bunch of horses right alongside the meadow. The pilot circled, and soon the cowboys appeared. The run was on.

The first thing that went wrong was I discovered my stomach was not designed for tight circling. After a few eruptions from that area, I finally got so I could see again, and I watched from above.

Four cowboys started the horses running, and after a bit one cowboy's horse went down in the snow. He wasn't hurt, but by the time he got straightened up and back on board, the others were long gone.

The next thing we noticed from above was that the cowboys chasing the horses seemed to be a little disoriented. (Cowboys don't get "lost," but they do sometimes get "confused" or "disoriented.")

They were running in fairly thick Jack pine and doing a fine job of staying with the bunch. However, they thought the wings were closer than they were, and they tried to head the horses to the right. Fortunately, they couldn't make the turn and the herd went into the wings, ran about a half-mile father and straight into the funnel—and of course, on into the corral.

Some days, although very few, you luck out. We captured 32 head on that run.

Once back on the ground, I stayed as close to it as I could for many years.

※

John Dodd, head rider for the Gang, and I took a little ride to find some horses that had broken off from the herd during this run. They were easy to track, and we wound up on the face of Saddle Horse Mountain. This is open country, and it was cold. I believe this day was the coldest weather I was ever out in.

It wouldn't have been too cold if the wind hadn't come up. We figured it was minus 36 degrees Fahrenheit with a 30-mile-an-hour wind blowing. I had been feeding or riding in weather as cold as 59 below, but not with a wind.

John and I had stopped for some reason, maybe to discuss the weather, as the subject was bound to come up. He was facing me and into the wind. I had my back to it, and had a silk scarf protecting me from the top of my nose to the base of my neck. As John was telling me about the coldest he had been, I witnessed his face freezing. I never knew that in these conditions, the face freezes in streaks— white streaks. I watched it happening, not realizing at first what was going on.

"John, I think maybe your face is freezing up on you," I interrupted. He rubbed his face a bit with a mittened hand and never stopped telling me about his other cold experience. I was glad he didn't quit sharing his story because it was a good one.

He was riding over in the Redstone area, which is known to be one of the coldest places in this country. I could remember hearing about it being minus 70 degrees there when it was only 59 below at Big Creek.

John claimed the worst part was that there was a 15-mile-an-hour breeze blowing. He was riding into the wind, so he got off his horse and started leading it down the trail. John was walking backwards, and after a bit he sensed something was beside him. John looked down to his right, and there was a coyote walking backwards on the same trail. Now that is cold!

Cecil Henry was one of the top cougar hunters and guides around. He had a few great dogs to help him out, and even taking me along wouldn't slow him down once he was on a track.

COUGARS

Cecil Henry and his family lived farther up Big Creek from us. One of Cecil's main pleasures in life was hunting cougars. He kept a few hounds and did pretty well in the winter because he got a bounty for them and then some more for the hides.

One winter a cat came into the Scallons' place downstream from us and killed a yearling heifer. It was a fresh kill when Pat Scallon found it in the morning as he went out to feed. He went home to get a rifle and was back about 20 minutes later, and the same cat had killed another yearling. The cougar wasn't hungry; it was just having a good time.

Pat got a message to Cecil about the cougar, and plans were made to go after the cat. Cecil asked me if I wanted to come along, and we made a deal. He would supply the hounds and a vast knowledge of cougar hunting and I would supply the horses and take an old one-ton Jeep to move a camp down to the Jameson Meadow cabin, which would be our base.

We chained the Jeep up all the way around and took off. Cecil rode and I drove. I had picked a big old wide horse for Cecil and a skinnier one for myself. I had cowboyed with Cecil and guided for him, and he was some hard to keep up with in the timber if he was in a hurry. I figured that wide old horse would slow him down in the trees, and on my skinny horse I'd have no trouble keeping up. Wrong again! He was still tough to keep up with.

We arrived late in the day and made camp in the old cabin. It was fairly dark, and we decided we had better have a look at the battery in the Jeep to make sure the fluid was up, because it could be hard to start if it turned any colder. I took one cap off the battery but couldn't see any fluid, so I lit a match and held it over the hole for a look.

Another lesson learned the hard way. It exploded and blew acid into my eyes. About two weeks before going on this hunt, I had read about a mechanic who had saved another mechanic by sucking the acid out of his eyes. They did not say why their battery had blown up, but I had learned one way to make it happen.

I said to Cecil, "Quick, suck my eyes out!"

Cecil sucked and spit, then changed eyes. After doing this for a bit, we chopped a hole in the ice and I shoved my head under water and opened my eyes to rinse them out. The acid wasn't stinging too bad, but Cecil hadn't shaved for about a week and the area around my eyes smarted a little.

We bedded down for the night and got going in the morning fairly early, heading towards Saddle Horse Mountain. My eyes were a little blurry at first and milked over, but by about noon they were back to normal.

We had three cougar hounds with us: Chief was black and tan, and was the veteran cougar dog; Pete was a Bluetick coonhound and Payday was a young Plott hound. We ran onto a track at Summer Range Creek, and Chief shoved his nose down in the track until he was in up to his shoulder. His tail started to wag slowly, and he went to the next track, doing the same thing: shoving his nose to the bottom to get the best scent. The other two dogs fell in behind, following Chief's example, trying each track. By now, all the tails were wagging faster and faster.

We were getting close to the timber on Saddle Horse Mountain when old Chief started to bay. Cecil figured the track was about 10 days old. The cats do not do a whole lot of travelling when there is so much game handy, so we figured it wouldn't take us too long to catch up to the cougar, even with a 10-day head start.

The other dogs started baying, and soon Payday got in the lead. He was younger, and Plott hounds are fast tracking dogs. We were loping along by now to keep up. Whenever we hit an opening, the sun would kill the track a bit and the hounds would circle the clearing, trying to pick up the track wherever the cat left the open and went to the timber, again leaving a strong track.

During this run, we saw two deer and one point where the cougar had stalked a moose. The cougar had kept a big fir tree between himself and the moose and, when it got close enough, it started to run, still keeping in line with the tree. Then you could see where it had moved over a bit and made a mighty jump for the moose. It must have landed on the moose's back, and the wreck was on. There were signs of a bunch of thrashing around, and we could see where the moose had thrown the cougar off in the snow; there were some big gobs of moose hair where the cat landed. The moose took off in one direction and the cougar walked away in the general direction he had been heading all along. This moose got away, but we did find another one that didn't.

The dogs were quite a ways from us now, and we could hear them baying steadily. We would try to figure out from the dogs which way they were going, then we would cut across country, pick up the dogs' tracks and carry on. We went over the top of Saddle Horse Mountain three times that day and were heading towards the mouth of the Chilcotin River. The country we ran through wasn't too bad for underbrush, but there were a lot of steep gulches to go in and out of. It was about 8:00 AM when we first found the tracks and got started, and we covered a bunch of country in a hurry. About

12:30 PM we heard the baying quit, replaced by tree barking—that meant the dogs had the cat up a tree. As a rule, the dogs will hold it up a tree for as long as it takes you to get there. In all fairness to the dogs, you should get there as fast as you can: there is no guarantee what these cats will do, and they are capable of killing several dogs in short order.

When we arrived on the scene, they had the cougar up a big fir tree that was hanging over a really steep gulch. Cecil tied Payday up because he was a little gun-shy, but left the other two dogs loose at the base of the tree. Some cougar men tie up all their dogs for fear of having a wounded cat coming down and killing their hounds. Cecil's approach was to shoot the cat dead and, when it hit the ground, the dogs would jump on the cat and believe they killed it. This makes the dogs even keener the next time.

He had very good luck with this technique until I came on the scene.

This was a big cougar, and we figured he would make a good trophy. I was to shoot him, and what I was packing for a gun was a standard 7mm Czechoslovakian Brno. A shot to the head was not considered, as it would probably destroy the head for a trophy. We picked a black spot, right in the middle of his chest.

Cecil got back on his horse just in case I missed, which I did. The shot went around the cougar's chest and out the left front leg. This brought the cougar out of the tree and down into the steep gulch. Pete and Chief jumped at the cat, and all three went down the bank. I figured this would be the end of one dog at least, maybe two.

Surprisingly, the cat took off running again and even went up the bank and climbed another fir hanging over it. During this run, I snapped another shot and missed. The cat was making pretty good time up the tree, and I couldn't get a good shot. It was partway up, but its injured leg let it down; the cat fell again, with the same scene following. Both dogs jumped at it in mid-air, and they all went to the bottom. This time the cougar turned on the dogs and grabbed old Chief, and was dragging the dog in when I managed to shoot the cat in the eye. That was it for the adrenalin rush.

We had to pull each claw, one at a time, out of Chief, as they were driven in pretty hard, but the dog was convinced he'd got the cougar, and he was pretty wound up. Chief was a great dog, and he'd had a great day.

The cougar was about 200 pounds and 9 feet 5 inches long from tail tip to nose. Fortunately, the bullet never came out and didn't destroy the head.

Killing these sorts of animals is not a great feeling, as you grow to respect them, but it is a necessity when ranching.

On the lighter side, John Siebert tanned a cougar he'd got and put the hide on his truck seat. This was before he was married, and he was doing some courting at the time. He would put the hide on the seat so the grain of the hair was going his way, then he would corner hard and the girlfriend would slide up against him on the smoothed hair of the cougar. Of course, she would have a hard time sliding back against the grain of the hair.

Most of them just stayed put.

The kicker on this trick of John's was that he always came across as very shy around women.

Getting hauled in a sled was one of the kids' most reliable forms of winter transportation—you didn't have to wait for the road to be cleared and it was easier for the dog to pull a sled than for the horses to pull our truck.

GOOD TO BE HOME

One question I'm often asked is, "How do you raise that many kids with no electricity or water in the house?" My answer is, "You turn them loose in the spring and gather them up in the fall when the snow gets too deep."

The beginnings of our family came on January 21, 1951, with the arrival of our first son, Roddy. Phyllis went to her parents' home in Haney for the birth because it was much closer to hospitals and doctors.

In March, I went to Haney to bring them home to Big Creek. At this time, we had a one-ton, single-axle Chev truck with a stock rack on the back. Since Phyllis and I rarely went to town, we always shopped about eight months ahead, so we had a pretty good load of food for the trip home, and a dozen laying hens. The weather was good on the coast, and the trip looked like it would be a piece of cake, so we loaded up and struck off.

The weather started changing as soon as we entered the Fraser Canyon. By the time we got to Lytton, it was snowing heavily and getting colder. We came out of Spences Bridge, and the wind was getting stronger and the snow was drifting across the road bad enough that we had to put the chains on. We were not too concerned because this truck, when chained up, could get through a lot of snow. We were getting along just fine, but the snow was getting deeper and deeper. Eventually we pulled up behind an empty low-bed truck that didn't have any chains. The driver had come to a halt right beside another truck that was stuck going in the opposite direction. There was no getting around them, so we came to a halt too. This was about a mile and a quarter from Ashcroft Manor.

By now it was about one o'clock in the afternoon. It was getting colder all the time, and snow was blowing across the road. We could see what looked like a grader coming from the Manor, and we figured he'd be along soon. We had lots of gas and would start the truck and warm it up every so often as the temperature dipped to 16 below Fahrenheit. The blowing snow had built up to the top of the posts beside the highway, and it was cold enough to give the snow quite a crust.

The grader wasn't getting any closer, so by seven o'clock we decided to hike to some buildings that the government had built for their staff and were luckily occupied. These houses were just before Ashcroft Manor and not too much father ahead. The walking was no good: you could go only a few yards before dropping through to your armpits. I was carrying Roddy and breaking trail. Phyllis was still weak and was having a really hard time keeping up, so we decided I'd better get to the buildings as quick as I could, then come back to help her.

I knocked on the door of the first house I came to, and a young fellow answered. I handed him Roddy and asked if he would take him for a bit while I went back to get my wife. He was very good and agreed to take Roddy right away.

Phyllis and I made it back to the house in about half an hour. Our hosts gave us a warm meal and offered to let us stay with them until the road was passable. I never saw the grader, but about ten o'clock that night, a D8 Caterpillar was out front heading in the direction of our truck. I went out and walked behind the Cat, thinking it would get to the truck soon. The conditions were tough, even for a D8. The driver could only take a skim off the snow and push it aside, and then back up to pick up a little more and then push it off. The snow was frozen like concrete. The grousers on the Cat were not good, and it had no ice cleats. We got to the trucks at one o'clock in the morning.

We stayed with the young couple that night and took off in the morning, having no further problems until we got to Williams Lake.

Here we learned that Becher Prairie was plugged and would not be passable until the next morning. Our supplies were fine in the back of the truck; we could get feed and water to the hens, but they were pretty cold.

The next day we made it through to Big Creek, only to find the last six and a half miles of the road to our place snowed in. I borrowed a horse from Dick Church, rode home and brought back our biggest team and Helge Johansen.

Helge was staying at our place while we were away. He couldn't drive a truck, so we hitched up the horses to help tow the truck. Helge had to sit on the hood in order to drive the team. He didn't like this too much, because the hood was kind of slippery. Luckily, he was very athletic and soon got used to it, and we got home just fine.

We unloaded the hens into our warm chicken house, but they were all squatting like they were already laying. It took a few days for them to straighten up and walk around like normal. It was several months before they ever did lay an egg.

It sure was good to be home.

Many camps we stayed in when we were tracking cattle in the winter were a far cry from the luxury of this cabin on the Chilco Ranch.

MONTREAL COWBOY

In 1953 Phyllis and I had a young man come to the ranch in early February. I'm not sure why he came, but maybe it was for adventure or maybe to experience the romantic life of ranching.

That winter, when the young man from Montreal arrived, we'd heard there was a little bunch of cattle down by the mouth of the Chilcotin River. The Montrealer, Harold, had never been on a horse, and even though it was 30 miles to the cow camp above the river, he was young, strong and eager to come along, so we took off.

It was minus 30 degrees Fahrenheit with about 14 inches of snow on the level. Not bad conditions, really. We made good time and arrived at our cow camp just before dark, too late to go to the river that day. We lit a fire and a lamp in the old cabin and settled in for the night. While I was making something for us to eat,

Harold was having a look around in the cabin and spotted a hole in the window.

"What made that hole in the window?" he asked.

Now, this story really starts the previous fall. We'd had a group of deer hunters at our place and were hunting out of our cow camp, near the mouth of the Chilcotin River. One of the hunters, Ivan Wells, had just taken up bowhunting, and he was the first one we'd ever seen to do this.

The first night in our cabin, he pinned up his business card on the window frame, stood back with his bow and practised shooting at his card. He was a pretty fair shot, and some of his arrows came close to hitting it. After several shots, he drilled the card and started to puff up a little.

"That doesn't look that hard, let me borrow your weapon," one of his buddies said.

He took the bow and arrow, pulled back and let the arrow fly. The arrow went right through the windowpane, but not so close to the card. It made a neat little hole something like a bullet hole. The cabin already had enough holes in it, so we shut down the practice session and no more was said or thought about it until Harold noticed it.

"An arrow," I replied.

No more was said, but I believe he did a little thinking on it. The next day, Harold was pretty stove up and didn't want to go down to the river with me, so I left him alone in the cabin and took off to see if I could find the cattle. I hadn't been gone long when a friend of mine, Johnny Montgomery, rode up to the cabin, tied up his horse and walked right into the cabin. No knock—not necessary with friends—but it startled the kid a little to see this big Native fellow come right in and go to the stove for a coffee.

This young fellow had prepared himself for our cold weather. He had gone to a surplus store and bought some good heavy wool pants and a fur hat. The wool pants were blue with a yellow stripe down each leg.

Johnny surveyed this outfit and asked gruffly, "You Mountie?"

Harold quickly said, "No, no, no, not a Mountie!"

By now, I'm sure Johnny knew he had a live one. "Where's Bruce?" he asked.

"He's gone to the mouth of the river, but he will be back soon," claimed the kid.

Johnny knew I wouldn't be back that quick, or maybe even that day. He sat down and enjoyed his coffee, not saying one more word. He wasn't a big talker anyway.

We had a big pile of wood that had been left in the cabin for winter riding in the area. When Johnny had first come in, Harold had sidled over to the woodpile and started splitting kindling with the axe.

I arrived back at the cabin late in the afternoon after having found that the cattle belonged to the Gang Ranch; their men would take them their way once I told them where they were. By the time I got back, Johnny was long gone and nearly our whole pile of wood was split into kindling. Harold didn't want to let go of that axe until the crisis was over.

By this time, it had really warmed up and started to blizzard. When we looked out, the snow was blowing straight across the window. I told Harold we had better head for home right away, as we would be travelling in a broke-out trail. If we waited for morning, we'd be breaking a new trail for sure, and it could be really tough going, the way the weather was coming. He had a look of disbelief in his eyes, but that left after about four miles on the trail home.

The wind was in our faces, and when we looked up and into it, our eyelashes would freeze together. Before and since, I have never ridden in conditions that bad.

We arrived home early the next morning, put up the horses and the trip was over. Harold didn't do any complaining the entire time we travelled. As a matter of fact, he said very little of anything. I figured he was either numb, or he'd learned something from Johnny about not talking all the time.

Sometimes it was hard to find tracks at all when you were searching for animals in country this big, but Dick always managed to, and he could tell you how old they were, too, almost down to the day they were made.

SPRING OR SUMMER?

Years ago, there was an annual fall gathering of cattle. These would be cattle that wandered down into the Jameson Meadow and Summer Range Creek area. In this area there were only two fences—one was in the Jameson Meadow region, which fenced off the upper spring range for the Big Creek ranchers. The other fence was for the Gang Ranch horse pasture that overlooked Farwell Canyon.

There was no fence separating the Big Creek permits from the Clinton and District stock range, which was for the most part Gang Ranch. This was years before the government sent in their "range management program," so there was still plenty of grass.

Dick Church and I camped just inside the first gate of the turnout at Jameson. Sometimes gates were left open or fences went down, and cattle could get in there. Consequently, this was one of the first places we started to hunt. We hadn't gone far when we rode up on some dry mud on the edge of a pothole.

Dick was, without a doubt, one of the best trackers in this country. He took a look and said, "There are no cattle in here; these tracks were made this spring."

There were some good cattlemen on this trip, and some were also fair trackers. They claimed the tracks were made during the summer and fall, arguing that there had to be some cattle in there.

This turnout pasture was six and a half miles long on one side, and was bound geographically by Big Creek on another side and had a fence on one end, so it was a fairly large area to ride.

Dick never argued at all. He just turned his horse and headed back towards the gate. He motioned me to go with him, so I did. The others rode on looking for the cattle. They were not green peas, and they rode for two days and never found one cow in that pasture.

When we were riding back I asked Dick, "How do you know those tracks were made in the spring and not this summer?"

He was a very patient man, and he replied, "Well, because of the way a cow puts its foot down in the mud in the spring. We know that when the cattle were taken out of here in the spring, there was still frost in the ground. When cattle are walking on this type of ground with frost under it, the toe and the heel will be the same depth in the mud. In the summer, the toe will always be deeper in the mud than the heel."

Dick had sized up the tracks around this water hole, and there were no summer tracks. It always amazed me that anyone would ever doubt this man: even the Native people had nicknamed him "The Bleed Hound."

HAVE FAITH

Through the years that we raised our five children at Big Creek, we were very appreciative of the services we received from the nuns at Anaham Reserve. There was an older nun there who was a registered nurse with a world of experience. She could take care of most emergencies, and when she was finished, you could generally just go home and heal up. This meant a great deal to us because it was excellent help and only about an hour from the ranch (depending on the road conditions). To go to Williams Lake, the nearest town, it was a good three hours, and that was when the roads were at their best.

Fortunately, we got by pretty well when it came to accidents. There were broken ribs and two broken arms, a tea scalding, two bad horse kicks and one hand pinned to the chopping block. Not bad for seven people through thirty-some years.

There is a story that is told about a few of these nuns who were on a trip to Williams Lake. They had a little van they drove when they went in for groceries, or to take someone into the hospital if they couldn't handle the case themselves. This particular day, they were going in to get groceries. Someone had forgotten to fill up their gas tank, and they ran out at the top of Lee's hill, near Hanceville. Not far from the top was a ranch called the Slea place, so they decided to get some gas there. However, when they looked around the van, the only container they could find was a potty, which they kept there for little kids going to town. One of the younger nuns was sent to go for some gas at Slea's. She had no problem and soon came back with the potty full of gas. She had borrowed a funnel as well.

They poured the gas into the gas tank and were just about finished when an older rancher in the country drove up. He stopped and sized up the goings-on.

"I appreciate your faith, sisters," he said, "But I don't think that is going to work."

The nuns then got in, turned the key, the van started right up and they drove off to town.

Now this old rancher's family had been Anglican for centuries, but the old boy became a Catholic that day.

Since mail day was always a great day for visiting, we'd all try to fit into the cutter to make the trip down to the Church Ranch. Monty was a great horse for the job, as long as no graders came along.

MAIL RUN

Getting the mail up to Big Creek required a few different stops. The mail "stage" used to come into Hanceville on Fridays from Williams Lake. The stage would drop off the mail in Hanceville and then go farther into the Chilcotin. We always called it the mail stage, but through the years the stage was replaced with one of Hodgson Trucklines' three-ton trucks. From Hanceville, the mail was picked up by either Frank Witte or his son Duane and brought to the post office at Big Creek. The journey from Hanceville to Big Creek was dictated by road conditions; through the years, the mail came by democrat, sleigh, packhorses or pickup, depending on what shape the road was in.

The post office was on the Church Ranch, and most people in the area went for the mail once every week or two. Mail day was a day for visiting neighbours, and the mail lady, Rona Church, would serve tea and cookies or cake to everyone while they visited. Nowadays, I haven't noticed too much of this great tradition continuing.

One day in the middle of winter, our kids went up for the mail. It was a beautiful sunny winter day, not too cold, with about two feet of snow—a little more than average. They took our cutter, pulled by our old horse Monty. Roddy was driving, and all five kids were packed in, including Kirby, who was just a few months old.

Getting to the Church Ranch was no problem. They picked up the mail and loaded back into the cutter for the six-and-a-half-mile trip back home. All was going well as they climbed the first small hill, and then, over the top part of the hill, came a grader. Most of this little crew had never seen a grader before, and the old horse certainly had never seen one before either.

Though Monty was "bombproof," apparently he was not "grader proof." Just as Monty spotted the grader, the sun hit the blade and flashed the old horse. That's all he needed to decide he didn't want to be in this part of the country anymore, and he bolted up a hill to his right.

This sudden run along the hillside upset the cutter. The kids were all airborne, and the horse dragged the cutter upside down to the yard gate. The four eldest kids were fine as they had landed in the soft snow, but they soon realized Kirby was missing. They figured she must be under the sleigh, so they rushed down, and with the help of a neighbour, got the cutter back upright. Still no Kirby!

Back up the hill, everyone went and started rooting around in the snow, where they eventually found her buried in a soft bed of the white stuff, all wrapped up in her blankets. Kirby was still snoozing and didn't even know she had been in a wreck. The term "wreck" did follow her around for some years after.

Little experiences the kids had while growing up on a ranch were varied and plentiful, which I believe has helped them all deal well with life in their later years. To date, I haven't heard of any of them taking stress leave.

When you can fit into a bucket as well as Dee and Ryan, there's no need for a bathtub. We saved that for the chickens.

BATHTUBS AND CHICKENS

For quite a few years, we had to pack our water into the house from a little creek that ran through the barnyard. There were several springs on the home side that stayed open year-round, but only one was high enough to develop into a gravity-system water supply. We finally dammed the overflow from this spring and got water into the house.

What a great thing this was, as the family was growing and the Saturday night baths required a lot of water hauling. In the winter, we took turns in a round tub set up in the middle of the kitchen floor. In the warmer weather, the kids would move out to the back porch and bathe in five-gallon pails. This worked very well, but when we got running water into the house, it was much easier. After some time with this great luxury, we thought we would get "uptown" a bit more and get a real bathtub. The tub we got was a very heavy cast-iron tub with four stout legs and coated with white enamel. I believe this was one of the first bathtubs on Big Creek.

We did have one disadvantage, though, because we still did not have a hot-water system. To overcome this problem, we half-filled the tub with water and put a tiger torch (a new and very useful torch) on one end of the tub. The idea was to get the tub hot enough to heat the water. This technique seemed like a sure thing, but it was not. Unfortunately, the cast iron did not heat up; the direct heat from the torch started peeling the enamel off the inside of the tub, but it didn't heat the water.

We never did get a hot-water system, but we did find the tub was a great place to raise a bunch of baby chicks, which is how we used it from then on. The sides of the tub were too slick for the chicks to crawl out, and by the time they could fly, we had moved them outside. So if you are ever contemplating buying a tub, do it; they are great for raising chicks. In the meantime, we went back to using five-gallon pails and the tub in kitchen.

Most of the time we didn't have to worry too much about there not being enough grass to feed an extra horse.

JUST FOR A LITTLE GRASS

One of our neighbours was the Chilco Ranch. The ranch was a good one. It ran about 2,500 head of cattle and was well balanced, with early spring turnouts and lots of summer and winter range.

The Chilco Ranch changed hands a few times through our days in the Chilcotin, and it was interesting to see the changes each new owner and management would make. We were fortunate that the many and varied neighbours were good ones; life is good in the backwoods when everyone gets along.

One of the times Chilco was sold, the new owners brought in a fellow from southern Alberta, Tom Livingston, to take on the management. His entire life had been spent around sheep, cattle and dogs. He fit really well into the Chilcotin, and he certainly had some funning in his makeup.

Tom had been there awhile when someone came into the ranch one day and reported that a horse had been hit by a vehicle near the Davey Allen meadow gate. Tom jumped in his truck and drove up there to have a look. Sure enough, there was an old grey horse that had been hit, and it looked like it had a broken hip.

Tom went back down to the main ranch and phoned the RCMP. He explained the situation and suggested they come over and shoot it. The RCMP claimed it was quite a ways to come, and told Tom to just go ahead and shoot the horse himself; they would take the responsibility. Nobody around knew the horse, but it wasn't one of Chilco's.

Tom went to the house, got his rifle, put it on the floor of the truck and started driving out of the yard. Walking across the yard was Grant Hoffman, a young fellow who had just come up to the ranch to work; he hardly knew Tom yet. Grant was a very quiet, peaceful young man, about 17 years old at the time.

"Jump in," hollered Tom. "I'm just going up to the Davey Allen to see how the grass is."

Grant jumped in, and away they went. As they went through the pasture gate, Tom looked up and there was the horse with its head down, eating grass.

"Look at that bugger eating our grass!" roared Tom, and he bailed out of the truck and shot the horse.

Not one word was said after that. They made a little loop through the Davey Allen and then headed back to the ranch, where Tom dropped Grant off at the bunkhouse.

I don't think Grant had ever sworn before, but he said to the others in the bunkhouse, "Now that is one mean sonofabitch! Just for a little grass!"

He seriously considered quitting at this point, but he didn't. Grant went on to become President of the Cariboo Cattlemen's Association and co-owner and manager of one of the biggest ranches in the Chilcotin.

I didn't have the best reputation for accurately gauging the depth of some mudholes, or the thickness of the ice on some lakes. I'm not sure why . . .

PESSIMISM

I have long been considered an eternal optimist, while John Siebert was considered the ultimate pessimist. I believe I might have strengthened John's pessimism. When we came up to a mudhole, for example, his usual expression was, "Uh-oh, we'll never make it." And I'd say, "Now, John, it's got to have a hard bottom. I'm sure that hole has a hard bottom. Let's take a run at her." We'd take a run at it, and I'd bet that 85 percent of the time I was wrong. However, in all the times we travelled together, the things we did together and the problems that we had, never once did he ever say, "I told you so!"

For example, one time we drove out of Big Creek in a four-wheel-drive Jeep that he owned. He was going with me to pick up a colt that I had bought from Ronnie Thomlinson over at the company cabin on the Riske Creek side of the Chilcotin River. This was in February, and we'd had some cold weather. On the way we came upon a lake, right in the middle of the road. There had been a thaw earlier in the winter that formed these lakes all over the place, and then of course they froze up.

When we came to the lake, John said, "Uh-oh. You know, we'll never get across it. You can't trust that water out on the range like this."

"John," I said, "It's been 50 below; we've had at least two weeks of 30 below and colder. That thing will be frozen solid to the bottom."

"Well," he said, "you never know."

Naturally, I replied, "Well, come on, John. Let's take a run at her and we'll go across. It wouldn't take much."

We could have gone around, which would have meant cutting the fence. It wasn't our fence, and we'd have to repair it, and so on and so forth. So we took a run at it. We got about halfway across and, of course, the Jeep dropped right through to the bottom. Mind you, it wasn't very deep; it just came up to about—well, it covered the floorboards of the Jeep.

John never said what one would expect at that moment, which would be "I told you, by God." Instead he just said, "I think I've got an axe in the back. We'll just have to get chopping." Which we did: we chopped for two hours to get back out of that hole. Then we had to go around and cut the fence anyway.

We finally arrived at Ronnie's, and while having a cup of coffee, I got to looking across Farwell Canyon and thinking about how, if we could make it up the other side, it was only about 16 miles home. To return the way we had come, we would have about 7 or 8 miles to get to the highway, 30 miles on the highway to Lee's Corner, 21 miles to Big Creek, and then another 6 miles into our place. That was a lot of miles! The other way just meant getting across Farwell.

In those days, it was basically just a goat trail through there; an old wagon trail is all it was. John figured we'd never get out of there because it would be sheer ice, to which my reply was, "Jeez, John, we've got a four-wheel drive." Four-wheel-drive vehicles were fairly new to us back then, but I thought that you just couldn't sink a four-by-four. We had chains to go all the way around; all we had to do was stick those chains on and climb straight up a mountain. So I talked John into it. He stipulated that he would not ride in the Jeep going downhill, or going uphill, and he would have nothing to do with driving it, even though it was his Jeep, so I agreed to drive it down in there. We loaded up the colt in the little horse rack on the back, and off we went.

We didn't have too much trouble getting down into the canyon, and while I was messing around with the chains or something at the bottom, John walked up the hill partway to see what it was like. I took off up the hill, passed John, and then the hill started getting steeper and steeper. Then, of course, the inevitable happened: I spun out with chains on.

I don't know if you have ever experienced spinning out with chains on, but it's kind of a hopeless feeling because your brakes don't do you any good, and once you start your momentum backwards, which I soon did, there's really nothing that's going to stop you. You're going to go down.

I went backwards down the hill, heading straight into the river. The Chilcotin River was a little tough swimming right there, especially in the cold weather. Being the kind of guy that John was, even though it was his Jeep, as I went by him I could hear him say, "Let her goooo!" In other words, JUMP!

Well, I had just paid ten dollars for the horse in the back and there was no way I was going to lose that ten dollars, so I stayed with the outfit. There was a little bit of dirt at the bottom, and I'll tell you, it wasn't much, but it was just enough. I had the Jeep in forward gear, spinning the wheels very slowly to try and gather some traction, but I didn't get any until I hit that dirt at the bottom of the hill, which did stop me. It shook me up pretty good; my foot was shaking so bad I could hardly use the clutch.

Then we had to turn around and try to go out the other way. I got partway up the other side, and the same thing happened: the Jeep spun out. I came down the hill backwards a second time, and this time, if I had gone over the edge, I was going over a cliff before I hit the river. (Of course, if I went over the edge, I was going to be in trouble anyways.) But, once again, the truck stopped right on the edge. By then I didn't feel much like driving anywhere.

Again we took out the axe, went into the bank and cut some sand out of it and sanded that hill. It took a long time. We must have been two and a half or three hours sanding just the wheel tracks up that hill far enough to get over the steepest part of it. Once we got over the steep part, the chains took us up the hill. Then, of course, we had to go the long way home and, boy, we got home late. The colt was rattled around a bit but it did make him into a good horse to haul. Nothing bothered him much again.

And not once did John Siebert ever say, "I told you this was going to happen."

A few cows and horses might not leave much of a mark on the road, but when 600 head pass through, it's another story.

HOW'S THE ROAD?

In addition to never saying "I told you so," John Siebert also had a pretty dry sense of humour and, most of the time, he was right about everything. I recall a time when he and I managed to get into a deal where we had quite a few cows. We must have had about 600 head between the two of us, and we had some good dogs too, which was a great help.

One time we were trailing these cattle down a road that was hardly ever used from the upper turnout to the Big Creek upper range. It was muddy, and the cattle churned it up just like digging a stick in a bucket of mud; it was kind of tough to get through. I had the lead bunch, and be-darned if I didn't come upon this guy parked on the side of the road in a car. You rarely saw a car up in that country, because it wasn't even good truck country, but this guy had come along and he was headed for the Scallon Ranch.

"How's the road?" he asked me.

By this time, I had been in this country quite a while and I had developed an attitude about roads. I figured if you could get through, the road was good. If anybody ever asked me what a road was like and I had got through, well, it was good, I told them. If I didn't get through, then I wouldn't even be there to answer the question. Or, if I never made it and I was walking, well, then, the road was no good.

I never thought too much about it. I just figured he might get through all right, so I said the road was good enough and I went on with the lead bunch. By then, the cattle were all strung out for quite a while, and the guy waited for a bit. Then along came John with the drag.

The parked fellow asked John the same question: "How's the road?" To which John replied, "What road?"

The fellow said, "The road you just brought these cattle over."

Then John said, "There is no road here. I came through and my stirrups were dragging in the mud. There is no way that that outfit of yours will ever get through there!"

"Well, that's funny," the fellow said. "You know that guy up in the lead there, he said the road was good."

"Mister, you just met the biggest liar in the Chilcotin," stated John.

I don't know that I was lying. I just figured the guy might get through. Well, I guess he didn't want to turn around, so he took a run at it, and he didn't get through. He was about a day and a half getting unstuck.

Like I said, most of the time Old John was right.

I suppose if the only person you have to talk to is your echo, you get used to waiting a while for an answer. Maybe that's why so many of the old cowboys talked so slow.

SLOW TALKERS

Even when John Siebert was a young man, everyone referred to him as "Old John." He was no older than me, maybe six months, but when he was 28 or 29, people were already calling him Old John.

Billy Woods was another genuine dyed-in-the-wool cowboy character who was born and raised in this country. They tell a lot of stories about Billy, and he was probably one of the better cowboys ever produced in the area. He was a great wild horse hunter, and apparently he could rope horses in the timber about as good as anybody who ever tried it. He used to do a lot of wild horse roundups with such great guys and great cowboys as Jim McDonnell and Bill Mulvahill, who were both very good hands.

A lot of these people lived their lives in such a way that there was no hurry in what they were doing; they didn't move around too fast, and they also talked slow. Billy talked very slow, and I noticed, as John got older, he also started talking slower. There was nothing wrong with that.

I remember John telling me one time about meeting up with Billy Woods in Williams Lake, and he asked where John was staying. When John said he didn't have a place yet, Billy told him that he had better come stay with him at the Lakeview Hotel.

"I've got two beds, and you can come and stay with me," offered Billy. Billy was a big man, and in those days, if you had a room with two beds in it at the Lakeview Hotel, it didn't mean you had two big beds. They were just like little army cots; they weren't very wide and they weren't very long. Also, Billy had forgotten that he had already asked Bill Mulvahill to stay with him. Bill Mulvahill was also older and was a big, stout man. Both Bills had to be at least 20 to 25 years older than John. When it came time to go to bed and they all got together in the little room, these two older guys had a discussion, and one of them says, "Well, we better let Old John sleep in that bed and we can bunk down on this other one."

It was pretty narrow on that bed, but the two settled in. John said he was just about to drop off to sleep when he heard Woods say to Mulvahill, "Say, Bill, what ever happened to that bay mare I traded you?"

This took quite a while to get out. John lay there for a while listening for the reply, and he thought Mulvahill had gone to sleep. John was just about ready to doze off again when he heard Mulvahill say, "She died."

You might not see someone walking on the open range very often, but the view is often just as good from your feet as it is from your horse.

CHILCOTIN LOGIC

John Dodd, cow boss for the Gang Ranch, and Jim McDonnell, who was breaking some colts for the Gang, were out looking over the summer range. There had been a report that some of the wild bunch of horses from Burnt Meadow had drifted out this way. Small bunches that break off from the main herd of wild horses can be a nuisance, as they are nearly always led by a young stud that will pick off a few mares from a domestic herd if given the chance.

They had been riding for a while, and they came upon old Anyhow riding out there. Anyhow was Alex Kalelest, a rancher who owned a place at the end of Home Ranch Valley on the Gang Ranch. He was a good cow man who wintered his cattle to come out in the spring in better shape than any in the country. The nickname "Anyhow" came from the fact that he could hardly say a sentence without sticking the word "anyhow" in there somewhere, anyhow.

Anyhow was a great guy and a very good visitor. He, John and Jim had been sitting on their horses for about an hour, talking things over. Jim looked across country and said, "That looks like someone walking back there." Someone walking on foot over the open range is something you would next-to-never see.

Old Anyhow never even looked back; he just said, "That's my woman."

"How come you're riding and she's walking?" John asked.

"She got no horse," Anyhow replied.

When you looked at our place from above, it was
pretty easy to count all of our neighbours.

BUSHED

If you ever consider going into the backwoods to live and
raise a family, one of the first things that you had better
check is that your partner can hack it back in there. Phyllis certainly could. She raised five children and had no real problems,
despite not having much in the way of facilities to help. We had
a few accidents, which you are bound to have with animals, kids
and farm equipment.

I'll never forget one time when Dee, who was riding from a very
young age, got bucked off a horse. She was riding bareback going
down a hill, and the horse started bucking and threw her against the
log fence.

This knocked Dee out completely, so we took her to town.
Williams Lake was 96 miles away over rough roads. Of course, she

woke up before we got her to town, but we wanted to get her checked out, just in case.

The folks in Williams Lake wanted to keep Dee in the hospital to check her out thoroughly. She was just a little kid then, I don't suppose more than about seven or eight years old. We did have a phone by this time, so we decided it would be best to leave her there and get back to the ranch.

The phone line was quite a set-up, going up in the trees and along the ground. It hooked onto the fence at Chilco Ranch, and it went for about four or five miles, just on the top wire of a barbed-wire fence. But the line did work, and I think it worked about as well as some phones do today.

Anyway, the first few days, we phoned into the hospital and asked if Dee was ready to come home, and they'd say, "No, we want to do a few more checks on her."

Pretty soon I started to get worried, and after four days I said to Phyllis, "We better go to town and see what the heck is going on. She just got a hit on the head, and she should be ready to come back."

When we arrived at the hospital, they told us that Dee couldn't talk. They had no sooner told us that when she came around the corner and spotted us. She came running up, and she wouldn't stop talking, telling us about all the things that she had seen in the hospital.

We hadn't realized that our children were getting "bushed." It's something that happens to kids in the backwoods. It doesn't hurt them any, but it makes you realize that you have got to get them out and socializing with other people, at least once in a while. That's all her problem was. She told us the nurses had asked her if she wanted to go see the little babies, and she really wanted to look at those little babies, but she wouldn't say a thing. Because of all the strange people around, she wouldn't open her mouth to say "yes."

She has never had any problem talking since, that's for sure.

We started trying to get the kids out a little more and seeing other people after that. Our roads improved through the years, and as the roads got better we received more visitors, so being bushed was never much of a problem again.

Moose might make decent company for horses,
but I'm not sure they'd be as logical.

MAUD: NO RUNAWAY HORSE

Not too many horses get the runaway idea into their head. This was without a doubt something that never entered Maud's mind. She was a fair-looking mare, about 1,400 pounds and ideal to pull a rake all day. However, pulling a rake all day was not to her liking: she expressed her distaste with this schedule by pulling for about three hours and then coming to a halt. Getting her started again could be quite the chore.

One particular day, Gay, our middle daughter, was driving Maud and another horse. They had finished raking one field by noon and were on their way to another field. They had to go through a gate to get to the next job, so Gay got off the rake, went around to the front and opened the gate. When she climbed back on, Gay gave a little cluck to go through. The other horse tried to move, but Maud had taken root.

Roddy came along driving a hay sloop with his team, and together they tried everything to get Maud moving again. They started with one leading her with the halter, and the other giving some kind suggestions to the horse while doing some line slapping on the butt.

No effect whatsoever. The kind suggestions developed into outright threats. I'm pretty sure our kids never swore at Maud, but they might have come close. After some time they were getting tired, but Maud still was not moving. Roddy had a pitchfork on the sloop, so he grabbed that and poked Maud with it. A pitchfork will move most animals, including bulls, but not this balking horse.

Roddy and Gay eventually sat down for a bit and discussed the situation as they rested up. Looking around for a solution, they finally decided on something else to try. They gathered up a bunch of dry leaves and little sticks and lit a fire right under Maud. She didn't budge for a bit, not until the hair on her belly was starting to smell like a branded calf.

Maud then moved out like nothing was wrong, and for years she rarely tried that trick again—at least, not very often. When she did try it out every once in a while, all you had to do was start gathering leaves and she would move out. They say animals don't have the power to reason, but I think ol' Maud was a reasoning horse.

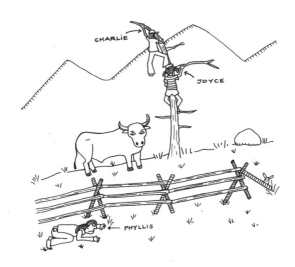

CHARLIE'S BULL

One fall we got a call from the Bell Ranch to tell us they had corralled one of our bulls. We got the call at night, and the owners said they wouldn't be home the next day to give me a hand. They also warned me to watch this bull, since he would charge a horse.

The next day, I went to get the bull and I packed a pitchfork along. Most bulls will show a little respect when introduced to a fork—not all of them, but it worked on this guy, and after one poke he was easy to handle.

I trailed him out of the Bell Ranch near 2:30 that afternoon. As I approached the Big Creek school, the kids were getting out and heading for home. The Bambrick kids were walking strung out along the road, about two miles from home.

Phyllis Bambrick was in the lead, and I hollered to her, "Watch this guy—he's a little waspy." She immediately dove over the log fence alongside the road and hid, lying down beside the bottom log. Her sister climbed a nearby Jack pine.

Then there was Charlie. He picked up a wooden club from beside the road and said, "If that sucker comes near me, I'll knock him flat!"

Just then Phyllis lifted her head as she lay beside the fence, and the bull spotted her. It jumped sideways, let out a snort and headed straight at Charlie. The bull wasn't after Charlie; he was just getting away from what he had seen alongside the fence.

Charlie made a quick decision and a good one. He dropped the club and headed for the tree that his other sister was already half-way up. He was quick, and when Charlie got to where she was, he scrambled right over top of her and kept on climbing till there wasn't a whole lot of tree left—about three inches—and then he quit climbing. The tree was weaving back and forth, looking something like a trembling aspen in a stiff breeze.

The bull soon lined out for home, and we made pretty good time, but he sure watched both sides of the trail all the way.

Though Charlie couldn't get away fast enough from this bull, he grew up to be a top-notch cowboy and was one of the best to have along on a roundup or riding, or to doctor cattle.

It didn't matter if we were in tents or cabins, somehow the horses always knew how to get back to camp—oftentimes better than us. [HUNGRY VALLEY COW CAMP]

THE NAVIGATOR

All the ranchers with permits on the same range would pretty well always agree on a time to round up and sort. On these roundups, you often had a very mixed crew: there were always the regular hands who worked on the ranches, and there were also often a few guest riders. The guest riders were usually some city folks who wanted the experience of a ride into the mountains to gather cattle. Generally, they were very helpful and good to have around.

One fall, our ranch was running some cattle jointly with Dick Church on an area called Fire Creek Range. When it was time to gather the cattle that we were going to ship to market, our guests were varied and all good help. There was Karl and Rita Seibert from Williams Lake; they were both good riders and a pleasure to have along. Then there was Hap Edmonson, a fellow from Sardis, BC, and his friend, Oliver Wells.

We knew Hap well, as he was a good friend of our family and had been up to the ranch many times. We did not know Oliver, however, but we'd heard of him, and I knew some of his brothers. He was in his early 80s, and we were a little apprehensive about him joining us, as these rides were not exactly a walk in the park.

Oliver owned a good farm in Sardis, and it turned out that he was a real hand. He always made sure there was kindling split and wood ready for morning. If we were short of water in camp, he'd pack some in. Oliver had his own old saddle, and we had given him a pretty good horse. He looked after that horse like he owned it. Oliver was, without a doubt, one of the best kinds of cowboys you could have in your camp.

Hap was also a great guy to have around. He could ride a little and had quite an outlook on things around him. Hap and Louise, his beautiful wife, had done some sailing off the BC coast, and as he progressed in sailing, he had wisely decided to take a course in navigation.

Hap had just finished this course before coming up for the roundup, and his first announcement when arriving at the ranch was, "I have just finished this intricate navigation course, so if on this roundup you get confused as to where you are, just look me up and I will pinpoint your location." It made us all rest a little easier in our minds to know we had someone with this capability travelling with us.

We all got into Fire Creek in good shape, set up camp and were ready to take off in the morning. The corrals and holding pasture were about six miles from our camp. We had not ridden far when we spotted a little bunch of cattle to our left at the start of a draw. Dick suggested Phyllis and Rita could get behind them and drive them up the draw, which came out at the corrals. Hap suggested he had better go with them in case they got lost.

"Have at it," said Dick, and away went Hap to join the girls.

We had a good morning picking up a large bunch of cattle before meeting up with the girls at the corrals.

One of our first questions to Phyllis and Rita was, "Where is Hap?" They claimed they hadn't gone very far, and Hap decided he'd better ride over the draw to have a look-see if there were some cattle over there. They never saw him again, and he never appeared all afternoon.

Around six o'clock Dick asked the girls to go ahead to camp, and we'd all be along in about an hour or two for supper. So they took off back to the Fire Creek cabin while we stayed and worked the cattle some more; but still no Hap.

I wasn't too worried about him, as it would soon be dark and I figured those navigators work off the stars somehow. Also, I knew if the stars were clouded over, he would know to turn the horse loose and she'd bring him back to camp. Just before dark, we saw him way at the end of the opening, just a jiggin' along, heading our way.

Upon arriving, Hap looked around and asked, "Where are the girls?"

"Don't know," Dick replied. "We left them with you."

After this comment, Hap turned in the saddle a bit, looked back the way he had come, put one hand over his eyebrow and had a hard look. I thought this manoeuvre must be the same one Christopher Columbus would have used looking for land after nine months on the sea. Or maybe Hap had learned it at that navigation school.

Hap told us what had happened to him after he left the girls. When he went over the little ridge and rode a ways, looking for cattle, he ran onto a little bunch of 12 head and started them in the general direction of the corrals. He probably wasn't far from hitting a trail to where he wanted to go; however, the cows sidled left and he missed the trail back to us and kept on driving all day. He pretty well drove them to the Snow Mountains. Hap said he knew he was in the wrong spot when he could hear foghorns from the Vancouver harbour. Finally, he gave the little mare her head and she jigged straight back to the corrals.

Upon hearing Hap's experience, Dick said, "It's getting late, so we had better head back to camp."

"We can't leave those women out here," exclaimed Hap.

"They will probably show up after a bit," said Dick. "If they aren't in by morning, we'll poke around a bit and see if we can cut their track."

For the six-and-a-half mile ride back to camp, Hap developed a slight crick in his neck from looking back.

We arrived at camp, and there were the girls. We were all so happy and relieved, especially Hap. I'm not sure anyone ever told him what happened, but all was well and our supper was ready.

Through the years, and the many people we rode with, Hap was one of the very best to take along for company—you just had to keep a lookout for him.

The cattle he had driven off with were picked up by the Gang Ranch riders at the head of Tosh Creek. We got them back that winter when we exchanged strays.

RUNAWAYS

We never had too many runaways throughout the years. We'd had a few with horses that we were breaking, but we generally had them rigged with a running W, a method that took the use of their front legs away, which makes it hard to run.

However, you can get in a runaway mode with a fairly well-broke team if circumstances develop that give the horses the notion that the answer to their problem is to leave the country right away. One summer, a couple of these situations did occur, one right after the other.

We were starting to hay at the time, and we were short one team of horses. So we hooked up Bud, a saddle horse, and Tex, the kids' horse. We were going to use them to pull a new dump rake we'd bought to bring in the hay. They didn't take to the rake very well, but they were very gentle and broke pretty fair.

I drove them the first day to see how it would go. It seemed to be going well, but after a bit I decided to adjust one of the tugs. Bad decision! To do this, you had to get off the rake and then get between the rake and the back end of the horse you want to make the adjustment on. I was just reaching for the tug chain to make the adjustment on the single-tree when old Bud blew a great deal of wind and leapt ahead—must have been stung by a hornet or something. Tex was always a follower, so he jumped ahead too.

I flipped over the back of the rake, and they were gone. The horses were gaining speed and got through three gates without hitting a post, and then across a narrow bridge in the barnyard. This bridge was just wide enough to sneak over carefully, and you had to be right in the middle to prevent dropping a wheel in the creek. Somehow they were perfectly centred and made it across.

Luck ran out as they pulled in close to a log fence. One wheel jumped the fence, and they dragged a bunch of logs off that fence. Then they reached the end of the front yard. This turned them down a hill heading for the house. En route to the house, they sheared off a little power pole, then one wheel hit the corner of the house, which somehow bounced the rake halfway onto the porch. The roof over the porch was held up with two support posts, which were quickly taken out, and the roof soon developed a sag.

We figured they were going at top speed when the rake on the one side picked up two galvanized-tin garbage cans at the end of the porch. They shifted up a couple gears, and then ran right into a grove of big aspen trees. This stopped them for sure, but it was Nightmare-Alice for the harness and rake.

We spent most of the night straightening out the wheels and harness. We had a D2 Cat at the place that belonged to the Wittes, and we would block the wheels in different places, then put the Cat blade on the hub and press it down. The rake had a bit of a wobble when we reassembled it, but it was usable.

The next day we went back to haying. I drove Bud and Tex for a while on the remodelled rake, and they were going just fine. Dee wanted to drive them, as Tex was one of the first horses the kids had.

"This team had a runaway yesterday," I pointed out.

"I know," replied Dee, "But they're going well now, and if they start to run, I'll just circle them in the field."

It was a big field, and she was a good hand with horses. I remember thinking that, the way the seat was on these rakes, if you fell off you would be off the back and clear of the rake. I decided to let her have her way, so she climbed on and away she went.

This turned out to be another bad decision.

Come to think of it, I've made quite a few questionable decisions.

Well, Dee was going just fine and getting a lot of hay raked. We were all doing well and settled into the day when one of the boys said, "Dad, there goes Dee."

The team was flying fairly low, and we could see Dee start to rein them in a circle, and all seemed relatively good. However, one thing we hadn't thought of was the irrigation ditches in the field. On the start of the circle, there was a ditch; when the team jumped it, the rake was airborne and Dee went flying. She did not go off the back, but landed in front of the teeth of the rake. The teeth picked her up, and away they went.

I hollered at the boys to get the rifle out of the truck, as I figured the only way to stop the team would be to shoot them. I was running towards the runaways when I saw them hit another ditch. Everything went flying, and Dee spilled out on the ground.

This all took place in an oat field, so there was a lot of dust and stubble. Dee was on her hands and knees shaking the dirt out of her hair, and I was still a long way away, but I could see one horse was running faster than the other, so they were making a circle and heading right back at Dee.

I yelled at her to look out. Dee dropped to the ground, covered her head, and the two horses ran right over her again. The teeth picked her up once again, and away they all went. They didn't go far this time before they hit another ditch, so Dee was shook loose once again. This time when Dee hit the ground, she took off running for the Jack pines. There was no way they were going to run over her again.

Dee went into the timber a ways and sat on a windfall. I finally got there and sized her up. She had a T-shirt and shorts on, so the stubble had scratched her up a bunch, but she had no serious cuts.

"Dee," I said, "that must have spooked you up pretty good."

"Well," she replied. "I wasn't as spooked as I was happy to get out of there. And the second time I was really happy!"

Some corrals were bigger than others, but it was usually easier to turn your horse around than to teach it to walk backwards. [GANG RANCH COW CAMP AT GASPARD LAKE]

DEPENDS ON HOW
YOU LOOK AT IT

Evan Howarth has been a cowboy his entire life. He spent most of his years riding for the Twin Rivers Ranch and Riske Creek Ranching. These two ranches are owned and operated together, making it one of the largest ranching outfits in the Chilcotin. A large portion of Evan's time was spent on horses, and he trained them for many years. Unlike some cowboys, he was interested in turning out well-trained horses, so he made a real study of it, and it paid off. Evan would go to any good clinic that came close to the area, and he learned from other trainers as well.

Sometimes Evan would take on outside horses, ones not owned by him or the ranch, to train for a fee or as a favour for a friend. He had a lot of cow work to do, and that can't be beaten as a training ground for young horses.

Evan was also a rodeo contestant and held his own in any competition. He taught his beautiful daughters to rope and ride as well, and they became good hands, both on the range and in the arena.

One day we were just sitting around and got onto the subject of horses. Evan told me about this big colt he was training for an old-time rancher from the area. This customer of his had some of the great attributes of the men of this country. He would take his time considering questions, thinking the situation over thoroughly before answering. Then he would answer slowly, and he was usually correct, unlike some people who talk so fast, they get way ahead of their thinking and knowledge and often give answers that do not come close to the question or situation at hand.

Evan was getting along well with this colt. It was reining around pretty fair and was comfortable with ropes and roping. However, what Evan was most proud of was the way he had this colt backing up straight with a very light line.

Well, one day the rancher dropped by to see how his horse was going. Evan got his colt in, saddled up and they went to the corral for a demonstration. Evan mounted up and showed where he was with the horse. He loped him around in a few circles, did some figure eights and stopped it. The horse was stopping pretty well by now, but not a word from the rancher.

Then came Evan's grand finale. He backed up across this big corral with hardly any pressure on the colt's bit, and backed the whole way across in a perfectly straight line. Evan was getting a little puffed up with pride from this last performance, but still not a word from the owner.

So Evan asks, "Well, what did you think of that?"

The ol' boy went into deep thought, and after a bit he slowly replied, "Well, if I had wanted to go in that direction, I'd have turned him around."

Although this was the end of being puffed up, Evan has a great sense of humour and he enjoyed that answer more than any other he could have been given.

BRAKES

Brakes were a luxury around our place. We started off repairing them, but the deep ruts and mud kept tearing the lines off. Soon we realized they weren't really that necessary, and all of our five kids learned to drive without any brakes.

The flat part of the roads didn't cause any concern about stopping as you couldn't build up much speed on them, and we never had much traffic—maybe 10 vehicles a year on our road. The rest of the traffic was horse-drawn, or people just riding by. (We did have one elderly lady on a bicycle who came into our place one time. I think maybe she was bringing us the Lord; he must have been giving her a hand, as it was some tough pedalling. She stayed with us a few days, and we straightened out her bike. She was a nice old woman and very good company. The boys even fixed the brakes on her bike.)

Gearing down was our answer to brakes, and when we were geared down to bull low but still flying down the hill, there was always the "turn-the-key" trick, which would get a little more "slow-down." Then the kids learned to size up the hill they were going down, and by cutting down the appropriate tree and dragging it behind the truck, they could get to the bottom just fine.

You can't, however, have five kids driving without any brakes and not have some interesting moments. One time Dee was driving, as it was her turn, and they were all coming home from our meadow up by Mons Lake in an old one-ton Chev we had. There was a pretty good hill about a quarter of a mile before you hit the main trail going home. The hill had a slight corner at the top and then went down this fairly steep pitch with another corner going left at the bottom. It was also narrow all the way down, with no room for passing.

Coming down this one time, they were doing a pretty fair clip, but Dee figured she could make the corner at the bottom with some help from the ruts in the road. She had just started down the hill and was committed to going on down when around the bottom corner came our neighbour Sherwood Henry.

The kids spotted him right away and started waving at him to go back. He thought they were just waving hello, so he waved back and kept on coming—until they met head on, dead centre. Fortunately, Dee hadn't built up too much speed yet, and they just had a little shakeup. Everyone climbed out to survey the damage, but aside from having to knock some mud off, there were no problems.

Sherwood said to Dee, "You wait till I see your dad and tell him what a wild driver you are."

Dee never was one to back down at all, and she replied, "You're lucky Dad wasn't driving; he'd have knocked your outfit right into the gulch there."

This all worked out okay, and Dee and Sherwood remained good friends.

There were a few times, however, when having no brakes did not work out this well.

One afternoon, I was not feeling too shiny and was lying down on the couch in the front room with no idea what the kids were up to. It turns out they had taken the old 8N Ford tractor to go up the mountain to get some fence logs.

I had made the road to get up that mountain, and it was quite steep. No one had been up it with a tractor yet. Roddy was driving, and his cousin Will Trethewey was sitting on one fender. Sitting on the other fender was a young boy called Harold Hendrickson, from Nova Scotia. Harold's folks sent him up to our ranch in the summers for a few years to get some experience. He was a good boy to have around, and he fit right into the ranch life. I'm sure he could have gone without this particular experience, though.

The hill started getting steeper as they went up, and the wheels started spinning. Roddy figured if he changed up to a higher gear, the tractor would not spin so much. However, he missed the gear and was in neutral going backwards down the hill. He cut the back end into the left bank, thinking this would stop the tractor. It did stop it, but the tractor flipped over.

Harold's leg was pinned under one wheel, and the tractor was over in such a manner that one of Roddy's legs was underneath, while his head was pinned under the seat. Will was thrown down the hill a bit, but he was unhurt. He took off running back to the ranch for help.

Will found me and tried to tell what happened. Will had a little stutter, but when he became excited, his stutter increased to such a point it was very hard to understand him. I finally understood that the tractor had flipped and Harold and Roddy were under it, but I thought he said a different road.

Anyway, I grabbed a jackall and took off running up the wrong road. Then, after finding out it was the wrong road, I went back down and got on the right one. By the time I got to the scene, things had straightened out amazingly well.

Luckily, the wreck happened on a really sandy part of the road. Harold had dug his leg out and then dug out Roddy. When I arrived, they were looking at the upside-down tractor and trying to figure out how to get it back on its wheels.

Harold was fine and, aside from being covered with quite a bit of oil, Roddy also seemed fine. His head did swell up for a few days, but then it went back to normal. He also had to use crutches, but only for about a week.

I figure we all used up a bunch of luck that day, and we were grateful it wound up the way it did.

Some years the school photo looked awfully similar to our family photo. L–R: Kirby, Dee, Ryan, Roddy and Gay

SCHOOL BUS

Schooling was not always easy in Big Creek. We were seven miles from the school, with a pretty tough trail to get there. Through the years, the kids had a lot of home schooling, but when the school was open, they would manage to get there one way or another. There had to be at least seven kids for the school to open. We did the best we could to open the school, but our family wasn't enough unless somebody hired a hand for their ranch who had kids. The school would open some years, and then a family would move out of the area and it would leave us short of kids again. However, if we could get it started in the fall with enough children, and even if after a month some moved away, the school remained open the rest of the year. Several times, our kids were the only ones in the school.

Getting to school was not really a problem, as they could ride or take the democrat, or the cutter during the winter. After a few years we got an old Austin pickup, and as soon as the eldest was old enough to drive, they used this little truck. Roddy was nine when he started driving to school. As soon as Ryan reached eight years old, he would take turns with Dee and Roddy driving the "school bus."

The boys saw a D2 Cat belonging to the Wittes, and they really liked the idea of a hand clutch, so it wasn't long before they put a hand clutch on their school bus. It worked just fine, but took up some much-needed room in the cab. The driver always had the most room, and the rest had to pile up a bit.

In the spring, when Big Creek flooded over the road, they took the old Ford tractor along and pulled their little truck across the flooded river. They'd just leave the tractor on the school side of the creek for the return trip home.

For the first 17 years at Big Creek, we had never seen a police officer come as far as our ranch. The odd time one made it as far as Church's place, but we never encountered any ourselves. The roads were tough, and no one really broke too many laws.

Then came the day when a policeman saw this little Austin truck go by the intersection at the Church Ranch, with seemingly no one driving. Ryan was driving at the time, and he certainly wasn't very big, which made him hard to see.

It was spring, and the road was just two muddy ruts to our front gate. The policeman was in a four-wheel drive and apparently had time on his hands, so he just followed the kids the six and a half miles home. Our crew never even knew he was there, since the little truck didn't have a rear-view mirror—not that they would have used it, anyway. Their drivers' education hadn't proceeded that far yet.

Well, they got to the front gate, and Ryan got out to open it. As soon as he got out, he spotted the policeman and immediately struck off running around the truck. However, he didn't get far, as the officer was waiting for him when he came around the front.

The officer asked Ryan how long he had been driving to school. At the time, Ryan was crowding 12, so he admitted, "Three years!"

We served the lawman tea and enjoyed some casual talk. Before he left, the officer said, "You know, I had to go into four-wheel drive twice to keep up to that kid."

There was no reprimand, just a pleasant goodbye and "good luck." We figured he must have been raised in the backwoods somewhere.

When things started to get a bit frosty and the days a bit shorter, television wasn't a bad way to pass the time.

TELEVISION

Red and Dionne Allison have been our friends for many years. Red was cow boss at the Gang Ranch for a few years and also had ranching interests on Big Creek. They lived in Riske Creek for a while, and now own and operate a place near Clinton.

Red and I had been doing some riding on the Gang Ranch near Big Creek, and Red came to stay at our place that night. Television had just come to the area, and we could get one station. After supper we sat down to have a look at this outfit. Red said he and Dionne followed this one series whenever they could get it, and that night it came in pretty fair.

The series was about a doctor who liked to solve mysteries. The mystery this night was that some woman had drowned in her bathtub. She was quite tall, and the doctor was having trouble figuring out how she had drowned, because the tub wasn't that long.

The doctor was mulling this over as he walked into his bathroom. His wife was having a bath at the time, and he was looking at her a bit when the solution hit him. His wife was lying on her back with her knees up, and she was about the same height as the drowned lady. The doctor explained to his wife he figured someone had lifted her knees up and this would allow the woman's head to go under the water. "Like this," he said, and to demonstrate, he lifted his wife's knees up. She accidentally hit her head on the tub, and down she went under the water and started drowning. The doc gathered her up as quick as he could, put her down alongside the tub and proceeded to give her artificial resuscitation. She woke up, all was well and the mystery was solved.

Dionne had missed this episode, and two days later, when Red and I arrived at their place, she wanted to know what happened that night on the show. Red gave her an account of the mystery, and I thought he was doing a fine job. Then came the part where she hit her head and went under.

Red said, "She was drowning, and the doc yarded her out, laid her by the tub and gave her artificial insemination."

Dionne just looked at Red for a bit and then said, "I bet that woke her up." I didn't realize for a minute that he had made a slight mistake in naming the procedure that the doc had used. It was actually a very understandable mistake.

Dionne could hardly wait for the next episode.

Who wouldn't want to catch a ride with the hay to the top of the stack?

TOYS

We did not think much about toys on the ranch, because there weren't any. However, throughout the years, toys did evolve.

The toy the girls loved the most was what they called "horse sticks." These two sticks were made from the abundant willows on the ranch, and they were the front legs of their imaginary horses. The girls would barrel-race one another, do show-jumping courses, go on trips around the place and, when they went in for lunch or the night, they would tie them to a hitch rail they had made outside the back door.

Roddy and Ryan made go-carts, which they would slide down the hills or tie to the back of the feed wagon or sleigh. The girls would drive the team and pull the boys out to the stack yard. The go-carts were designed to float through the mud in the spring, when the wagon would be up to its axles in mud.

One of the rigs the kids most enjoyed was our hay stacker. Throughout the years, we put up our hay many different ways, such as using slings and sloops (pitching the hay and building a load on the sloop, then stacking it with stack poles). Then we went to using sweeps and an overshot stacker. A sweep has a series of poles that slide along the ground and bunch up hay for transport to the stack yard where the hay is deposited on to the teeth of an overshot stacker or slide stacker to make your stack. A sweep can be powered with a horse on each side or in front of a tractor and the overshot was a method of throwing the hay up on to the stack.

At first, we used two sweeps and the overshot. We had a boy on each sweep, and they would load up their sweeps, drive them in and deposit their load on the stacker. The overshot would be powered by a team or pickup truck. By going up slowly, we could let the load kind of dribble to the back of the stacker and this was the start of one end of the stack. Then we could go a little faster and throw the hay into the middle of the stack. Finally, by going faster, we would throw it to the end of the stack.

We would have a "stack man" building the stack as it went up. He would keep the edges straight and hard. When the stack got high enough and we wanted to top it off, we would start forming a mushroom-shaped top. The rain or melted snow dripped off this cone, missing the sides of the stack.

The first year we built this stacker and started haying, the kids sized it up for a bit and soon saw there was fun to be had. Their idea was to get on the hay, get a ride up and get thrown out with loose hay onto the stack. This was very successful, and a bunch of fun was had. We all tried it, and everybody agreed it was a keeper activity.

Then came their Uncle Bill Trethewey to give us a hand with the haying. He often came up and was a great help and fun to be around. He observed this performance by the kids and rightfully decided that it was worth a go. The day Bill was due to launch, the pull-up team was needed in the field, so we switched out the team and replaced the horses with the kids' little school bus, an Austin pickup.

Well, Bill climbed aboard the stacker and started on his journey. Now this little truck could pull it up quite a bit faster than a team, so you had to throttle back a bit. However, throttling back wasn't about to happen. The kids figured they would give old Uncle Bill a memorable ride.

I heard a long, long holler and turned around to see this figure flying through the air, arms and legs flailing, and then he missed the end of the stack and disappeared.

Luckily, no harm was done. There was hay at the end that had also missed the stack end and Bill landed on that. Bill had a little hitch in his getaway, probably from all the flailing, and he was a little hoarse for a few days. Neighbours said they heard the holler, and they lived two and a half miles west of us. I never did find out who'd been driving the truck, though.

Some years were drier than others, and that could hurt the grazing some, but not as much as some of the government's ideas.

RANGE MANAGEMENT

Back in the '60s, the government decided to implement range management programs. I think the idea behind them was to somehow keep us from overusing our ranges so that there was always enough grass, or something like that. It wasn't news to us that we had to spell the ranges off every other year to give the grass time to grow back after a year's worth of rustling but, every so often, we'd have some guys from the government come in and check things out to make sure everything met their requirements.

One of the things these book boys started doing was counting our cattle. We were only allowed to have so many cows per acre. The idea was, if we applied for a 300-head permit and we really only had 250, then they would knock your permit back on that piece of land by 50 head and you would never get it back. Ranches were valued at $1,000 per animal unit, so if you lost 50 head, or if you were in trouble financially and had to sell 50 head, the value for your place decreased by $50,000. We all had good years and bad years, and in the bad years you'd have to sell more cattle than you planned just to make ends meet. To keep their permits up and their ranges filled to capacity, ranchers were forced to borrow money to keep the numbers up on the herds, or lease cattle, or fool the range detectives.

I'm told that fooling the range detectives is what the ranchers most commonly resorted to. One method of fooling them was to get one of these clicker people counting cows. (They were known as clicker people because they had to use a little clicker to count the cattle.) We'd gather the cows into one corral and let them out the gate into another corral, and these young people would click away as the cows went by.

This one fellow I knew fed the cattle in a pen behind his barn. When he knew the clicker people were coming, he moved the cattle to a set of corrals away from the barn and took the clicker people up there to start their clicking. It was always pretty close to coffee time, so someone would suggest they go to the house for a coffee. The last man out of the upper corrals left the gate open, and while everyone was having coffee, the cattle drifted down to their regular feed ground behind the barn and out of sight of the house.

After coffee, the clicker people went out behind the barn and counted the same cattle again.

I heard of another fellow who took the clicker people out on horses, and they'd all ride up to a meadow where he was rustling some cattle. They would ride into a little opening and the clicking would begin. Then they'd go to another meadow, and there'd be more clicking. After a little while, and a little circling around, they started going into meadows they'd already visited. The old rancher was using the old method of counting, you know, counting one, two, three, etc., in his head, and when he knew he was close to his permit limit, he just quit circling the area and rode on home.

These young people who came out were very nice, respectful folks, and I'm sure later in life they learned to count without the clickers and became good people.

Meadows are a great place to learn to drive, but they aren't always as flat as they look, which is a good thing to keep in mind when you're parking.

CRASH 4

It is a common practice for kids growing up on ranches to begin driving at a young age. Our youngest, Kirby, began driving at age four. That winter we were feeding our cattle at our Mons Lake Meadow, four and a half miles from the home place, and we would go up there every day.

We started the feeding with a team of horses and would drive up with a sleigh. All the other kids were at school, so Kirby would drive the team and I forked the hay off the sleigh. Later in the winter it warmed up, and we started using our little old 8N Ford Ferguson tractor instead of the team.

We would load up the sleigh rack with hay, and then I'd tie Kirby on the seat. I'd get the tractor going in low gear and low throttle, and Kirby would steer around the feed area. I would jump off the tractor, fork the hay off the sleigh to the cattle, and then I'd get back on the tractor. Kirby helped me with this job until she was six years old, when she too had to start school. She couldn't figure out how I would feed alone after she started school, and was upset about not having the job again that winter.

Kirby did a lot of driving in her younger years, travelling all around to rodeos with Dee. They hauled a camper on the pickup and pulled a two-horse trailer throughout BC and Alberta. She never did have much trouble, and she was driving in a lot of sorry conditions such as snow, mud and ice.

However, this situation changed somewhat when she got her driver's licence.

The first accident happened when she was coming out of the ranch and hit ice on a bad corner. She flipped the truck down over the bank and wound up upside down. There was a radio telephone in the truck, and she called the ranch to say she was upside down, wedged between two trees, there was gas was leaking out of the tank in the back and she couldn't get out.

I had just finished preg-testing some cows and was changing into different clothes, but all I had on at that moment was my underwear, shirt and socks. Another fellow and I jumped into another pickup and went fairly fast to the scene. Kirby wasn't that perturbed, but I was, and when I started down the bank, my feet slipped. I sat for the rest of the journey down, skidding on my ass. My underwear couldn't stand it and broke through to bare skin, which got some scratched up. Besides the pickup, this was the sum of the injuries received, so it wasn't much after all.

The next mishap was when Kirby parked the one-ton ranch truck outside the house, jumped out and went inside. The parking area she picked looked plumb flat, so it seemed reasonable that the truck would not move. This was an incorrect assumption, as the truck took off, headed for the house and then made a sharp turn down a very steep hill and hit an extremely large fir tree. The motor wound up on the front seat of the truck, but otherwise, everything was fine. At least, thanks to the tree, it didn't end up in the Fraser River.

The next, and almost the last, incident was when Kirby was driving in Williams Lake. She had just turned off Highway 20 onto Mackenzie Avenue, and she reached down to pick something off the floor that had fallen off the seat. When she looked up, she was heading straight for an old bus towing a Volvo. Kirby clipped the bus, spun around and sliced a narrow strip off the entire length of the car with her bumper. Two for two! There was very little damage to her pickup. The bonus came the following week when the local paper printed her mother's name in the article about the accident.

At this point, some of Kirby's friends and family chipped in and bought her a personalized licence plate that read CRASH 4.

Kirby is in fact one of the better drivers in the family, which doesn't say a whole lot for the family's drivers. Her experience has helped make her very calm and unflappable. She can drive my outfit any time.

BILLY WOODS AND
HIS HUNTING BUDDY

Billy Woods was one of the great cowboys who called the Chilcotin home. He had been in a typical bad accident when riding one time, and it left him with a bad arm and hand, but he could still play a fiddle, rope and ride with the best. He is said to have been the master at roping wild horses in the timber. This is not an easy feat, as the trees tend to get in the way and your target is ducking the trees and you at the same time. Billy's ability with a rope was quite a thing to watch. His arm and hand were a slight handicap when tying a calf, but he could still hold his own, and missing a calf was a rarity.

Like many ranch hands, Billy was a game guide in the fall to supplement his cowboy income. He had a hunter out one day, and this fellow was an ardent gun nut. The hunter loaded his own shells and was a very good target shooter; however, he had not done much—if any—game hunting.

During the hunt this day, they came on a fair-sized ridge. Billy suggested to his hunter that he go down one side of the ridge and Billy would go down the other side, and they would meet at the end. Billy talked very slow, as did many of the older cowboys—they had learned after a bit that there really is no hurry in life. By the time Billy finished his instructions to this fellow, the day was shortening up a little and so they split up and started down their sides of the ridge.

After arriving at the end of the ridge and not running into any game on his side, Billy looked for the hunter, who had not yet arrived. He went on down the side the hunter was to come up. He went quite a ways and then saw some movement up a tall Jack pine. It was weaving around a fair bit, and he could see his hunter perched up there, kind of bug-eyed. The hunter had come around a corner and nearly ran head-on into the first bull moose he had ever seen. He was so impressed that he dropped everything, including his rifle, and shimmied up the closest tree. This seemed like the best thing to do at the time, and by the time he was done climbing, there wasn't a whole lot of tree left.

The moose just wandered off a bit and looked back to watch this climb to safety. Billy put the moose down, as this is what they were there for. Then he looked up at his hunter and shouted very slowly, "Say, can you see any more from up there?"

I think Billy's question made the hunter feel better about himself. He probably felt this may be part of hunting: you know, climb a tree, look around for some game from up there, help your buddy on the ground, and so on.

BEAR CUBS

Uncle Bill Trethewey and I were looking for cows down on the summer range between the Sherwell place and the Franklin place. It was a great day in the fall, and we planned to spend the night at our lower cow camp at the mouth of the Chilcotin River. As we were going along, we heard a noise behind us that sounded like a baby crying. We turned back and rode towards the noise to see what it was.

A mother black bear and three cubs were running towards an island of willows. One cub was behind, and it was doing all the crying. The two cow dogs we had with us quickly treed one of the cubs.

The idea came to us to catch one of the cubs to take home to the kids for a pet. Dick Church had a bear he raised as a kid. He was about 15 or 16 at the time, and he had the bear for about four years. The bear would wrestle with Dick, and he would take it to all the dances on Big Creek. The bear became a very good dancer but would only dance with Dick. Maybe it was because it never got too many other offers.

The bear grew to a fair size. After a bit, it figured out where everyone was eating at the big house. The bear started taking stuff off the table, and keeping it out of the house was becoming difficult. Dick took two pieces of truck springs and bent them in such a manner that when they were bolted to the door frame, you could drop a two-by-eight board across the door on the inside, making the door bear-proof.

The big test came one evening when there was a big moose roast on the table for dinner. They could hear the bear on the porch, and hear the big pet testing the door a bit. Thinking they had outwitted the bear, they started to relax a little when there was a big crash. The bear had knocked the whole door frame out, along with the two-by-eight and the door. It then waltzed in, took the roast off the table and left.

That was it for a pet bear. They hog-tied the thief, put it in a wagon, drove the wagon up to a remote area 30 miles away and turned the bear loose.

Bill and I knew all this, but we figured that my kids could teach their bear better manners. First, though, we did have to get it out of the tree. The plan was for me to climb the tree, rope the cub and tie it on the saddle behind me, and go home. Bill was to stay at the bottom of the tree with his gun handy in case the mother came back. I left my hat with Bill because it would be in the way and started to climb with a rope to snare the cub.

The cub could see the rope coming and would duck behind the tree. Then it would turn upside down and come down the tree, snapping its teeth at me. Bill would holler and I would holler, and it would turn back up the tree.

I had no success getting a loop on it, and everyone was getting a little nervous, especially the bear. The stress seemed to get to the cub, and it relieved its stress on my head. The cub had been feeding on rosehips but, after passing through the cub, they did not smell anything like roses. Being bald made the situation worse: the stuff splattered off my head, odoriferous, hot and slippery, and ran down my neck.

By now, Bill was rolling around on the ground, seeming to think the situation was humorous. I was hoping the mother would return and chew a little on Bill. I was losing my grip on the tree (it was getting somewhat slippery), and I was gagging, so I changed my plan and returned to the base of the tree. We set a snare at the bottom of the tree to catch the cub, but it was not our day. As we reared back on the rope snare, the cub got away.

Bill rode upwind of me for the rest of the day, and the odour subsided after a week or so.

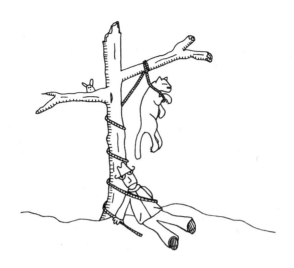

TRUMAN SHORTENS HIS ROPE

Truman Henry was a great hand with a horse. I've only seen two people in my time that had his way with horses—total insight and understanding between horse and man. Truman could talk a bad horse into a calm that anyone else would have had a wreck on. He had the same ability with dogs, so consequently he was generally well mounted and followed by a good dog.

One day he was going out on a known outlaw of a cayuse. A hand will never go out without a rope tied on, but will sometimes leave his rifle back if he's on a bad horse. This was one of those horses: bad. Sometimes situations come up, even on a half-bad horse, that may result in an interesting ordeal.

Truman had been riding for about two hours from his home when he came onto a fresh cougar track. There was around two feet of snow, and he was riding across Island Lake when he spotted the cougar that was laying the track.

He thought a bit about it. He had a new nylon rope on him that he figured could use some stretching to make it a better rope. He got off and tightened his cinch; you don't want to be roping a cougar with a loose cinch.

The cougar hadn't spotted Truman yet, so Truman shook out a loop and started closing in on it. Soon the cougar was loping ahead of him with some difficulty in the snow. Getting a good throw at the cat was difficult; the horse wasn't exactly cooperating. It might have something to do with the horse having its first look at a cougar. The horse could have been wondering, "If we catch it, then what?"

Anyway, after several passes and some gee-hawing on the lines, they were close enough for a good shot, and the cougar got roped. Truman dallied up, tying the rope hard and fast to the saddle horn, and then it was Nightmare-Alice time! When the rope came tight, the horse must have realized he was hooked onto a big cat and it was time to change countries.

Bucking and running, they hit the edge of the lake where, like a lot of the lakes in this country, there were lots of hummocks. By now the pony was moving along pretty quick, and the cat was air-borne most of the time. Soon it appeared the cougar was knocked out, so Truman rode up to a snag and threw one end of the rope over a branch. He took a hold of the rope and dallied up to the horn, figuring on hanging the cat until he could go get a rifle. Truman thought he had roped it around the throat, but the cougar actually had one front leg in the loop too, which stopped it from choking.

As Truman walked away, pulling the cat up to the limb, the horse saw the cat going up the tree and figured it had had about enough for one day. The horse really tied into it and bucked his buddy off. The dally came off, and Truman still had a hold of the rope. As a result, it swung Truman into the base of the tree and there he was—next to the cougar. Then he had to shimmy up the tree far enough to tie the rope off to hold the cougar till he could straighten out the circumstances that had developed in the last few moments.

Truman's horse had run off after unloading him, and it took some doing to get back on board to go home but, as I said, he had a way with horses and dogs. He made it home, got two good hounds and came back. The rope around the front leg had saved the cat from choking, so it came to, chewed the new rope off and got away. Not for long, however, as the hounds did their job well. Truman ended up with one cougar and one shortened rope.

Horses are good company for chickens, but they aren't the best guards.

THE WELL-FED LYNX

We raised a few chickens every year, some to eat and some to lay eggs. Things were going pretty fine, with the chickens roosting in the trees around the barn and the laying hens laying their eggs in the barn. However, one evening while Phyllis was plucking a chicken and I was in the back room, she hollered at me that something was after the chickens. I grabbed the rifle, which was by the back door, and went out, but it was getting dark and a little hard to see.

"Where is it?" I asked.

"Right down there in the barnyard!" exclaimed Phyllis.

I looked around, and after a bit I thought I could see some ears sticking up, so I zeroed in between the ears and fired. Something that looked like a lynx took off running about 15 yards from the stump I had hit. The shot in the stump wasn't a bad shot, but I had to take another shot at the lynx. It flipped up in the air and came down running. Our two dogs, a Lab-Doberman cross and a border collie, got in on the act and took off after the lynx, chasing it up by our outhouse.

The cat turned on them, and the wreck was on! The dogs got quite an education at this point on scrapping with a big cat. The lynx was having no problem handling the dogs, but they kept it busy. I ran to the house and grabbed a shotgun to help the dogs out. The three of them were scrapping for a while before I could get a clear shot without annihilating one of the dogs.

The next day we counted the chickens and ducks we had left. We figured we had lost about 20 chickens and 3 ducks. The lynx had been living well. We then built a chicken house and locked it up at night. It felt like civilization was moving in on us.

CHIVERIE

On Big Creek, we had a very popular young couple get married awhile back. She was a beautiful young girl from the coast, and he was a product of the Chilcotin—not beautiful, but a very handsome young man. The community decided to give them a chiverie, as is the custom in some cultures. They are a lot of fun and a good excuse for a party.

The way chiveries happen is that first, you let the newlyweds settle into their new home. After a couple of months, the goings-on get going on. The plan is for the chiverie to be a sort of surprise party that doesn't start until midnight because you need to give the couple time to settle down for the night. Then you surround their abode with fireworks, and the explosions start the party off.

This time we didn't have any fireworks on hand because no one had been to town for several months. Luckily though, some of us had some 70 percent dynamite for ditching powder. We cut the sticks in half, buried them in holes about 12 inches deep, and set the key charge with the fuse and cap. This key charge will blow and set off the rest at one shot, if you space the sticks about 18 inches apart.

We surrounded the cabin this way, stood back a bit and lit the fuse. There was a fair explosion, much louder than firecrackers, and quite a bit of smoke. The noise did wake the couple up, and we could see them peering out the window after the smoke cleared. They were surprised, and so were we, to see that the cabin now had a ditch around it, much like a fort in the Roman times. No harm was done and, after making a little bridge over the ditch, we all filed in and had a great party.

It is a wonder this tradition hasn't caught on more. Maybe that's because dynamite is harder to buy now.

How could you resist stopping in for a visit when you have three sets of antlers waving you in? That means that there are at least three good stories waiting inside the door. [CHILCO CHOATE'S HUNTING CABIN]

VISITING

I think young people today are moving around faster and doing everything quicker than ever with cars, or maybe even using faster horses or something. I don't think they are developing into the great old character who used to sit around a campfire and have lots of time to visit.

Visiting is something that is really getting to be a lost art. For example, we would never think of passing by someone's house without stopping and visiting. You just wouldn't ride by a guy's ranch without stopping in for a cup of tea or just to talk with him for a while. If you were driving down the road and you saw someone stopped on the side of the road, the first thing you would do is stop to see if he was having trouble. If he wasn't having trouble, then you would still have a visit with him. Sometimes you would spend an hour or two talking. We always seemed to have time for that.

Nowadays, guys will just drive on by. Some will wave, and some will stop to see if you are in trouble, but a lot of people just flat out don't have time to visit. I had that brought out to me one time. I had to go to the Gang Ranch to pick up a bull that had wandered over onto their range, and they had penned him in a corral. In those days you had to go around to Williams Lake, over the Dog Creek hill, drop down across the Fraser River and then drive down into the ranch. I left about four o'clock in the morning and went around the whole loop, so I got in there about eight o'clock in the morning.

The manager at the time was Wayne Robinson. Now there was a real hand. He had come up from the States, and he spent his entire life working cattle and horses. He was a great horseman.

When I went to pick this bull up, he said, "Before you leave, I want to show you some colts I've got here."

He had 64 head of colts. He knew how each of those colts had been bred, and he went through their pedigrees with me. That took quite a while; as a matter of fact, it took until about eleven, and then we had to have a cup of coffee.

Then he wanted to show me the yearlings. We went out, and I forget how many yearlings there were—probably just as many—but it was interesting. I really liked horses, and I liked the way this guy set up the breeding program. He was looking for good using horses. So, we went through those yearlings, and then, of course, he had to show me the mares. By the time we got through the mares, it was suppertime. I had supper with him, and by then it was starting to get dark.

I finally said, "Well, I've got to go. They'll be thinking I'm stuck somewhere and will be out hunting for me."

"You know, we are losing the art of visiting," he replied. I had visited with him all day!

He told me about going across Wyoming when he was a young fellow. He was driving about 16 head of horses, and he got snowed in by a blizzard. There was an old guy out there who had a small stack of hay and a little cabin that he was staying in for the winter.

Wayne rode down in there and he couldn't get out, so he fed this guy's hay to his horses. It was a month before he could move, and he had just about used up all the hay.

Finally he was saddled up, getting his horses packed and was ready to take this bunch and carry on down the road when this old guy comes out of the cabin and asks, "What are you doing?"

Wayne says, "Why, I'm getting ready to leave. I've got to get down the road." The old guy looked at him and muttered, "You know, if that's all you are going to visit, don't you bother coming back here."

Wayne had been with him for a month! I don't really believe in visiting for a month, but it is too bad that nowadays people don't do a whole lot of visiting.

The legendary Benny Stobie

GLOSSARY

11 good logs high 10–12 feet

ass-buster an uncomfortable saddle

bad road a road you can't get through

Bennett wagon a fine travelling wagon made from an old car, including the wheels, pulled by horses

burn a scar from a forest fire that has naturally started reforesting

bushed what happens when you spend too much time out in the backwoods without seeing many people. Sometimes it can make you forget how to talk.

chiverie a surprise party to celebrate newlyweds that generally takes place a few months after the wedding. The goings on get going on around midnight, once the couple is settled down for the night. You surround their house with fireworks (although dynamite can be used in a pinch) and the explosions start the party off.

clicker people the young people the government sent in to count cows on the range, also known as range detectives. They were called clicker people because they had to use a little clicker to count.

D8 Caterpillar a big tractor with tracks (grousers) on it and a large detachable blade like a bulldozer, used for clearing roads and straightening bent wheels

dallied up a way to tie a rope to your saddle if you're trying to catch a hold of something. There are two ways to dally up. The first is to wind the loose end of the rope around the saddle horn so that it can be released if you foresee a wreck. The other, and more common way, is to tie a rope hard and fast to the saddle horn. The disadvantage to this method was that if you roped something, you were latched on to it hard and fast, and it could become Nightmare-Alice time.

drag the end of something, like a bunch of cattle

dump rake a device used to rake hay and dump it in a windrow or bunch it for caulking later

give a horse its head letting the horse find its way back to camp without any direction from the rider

good road a road you can get through (although it may not be easy and may also be hard to distinguish from a bad road)

good using horse a well-broke, healthy, tough and sound horse. It's a good walker and has a good disposition, good confirmation and some natural cow sense bred into it.

half hitch a simple knot made from passing one end of a rope around something and through a loop. This type of knot can be used in a lot of different situations, including hog-tying animals.

hobble a device to limit the movement of a horse's legs. They can be made from a variety of materials but the point of them was to get horses used to having pressure on their legs. There are a few different styles of hobbles out there. *See also:* running W and Wyoming hobble.

jackall type of jack that is good for lifting heavy loads and can push things up higher than a normal jack

line slapping slapping a horse with your line(s), but if you were tired of living you could reach forward and slap them on the ass with your hand. Don't!

Nightmare-Alice time when the wreck is on!

overshot stacker a method of throwing the hay up on to the stack

range management a program introduced by the government in the 1960s to make sure that there weren't too many cows on the same piece of land. It was supposed to keep rangeland in good shape for years to come but sometimes it made things worse.

running W type of hobble that was used more for horses that were pulling things, like wagons. It had a rope from the wagon to the harness, and the harness was attached to the hobble around the horse's legs.

rustling out a term for foraging for food, usually grass. It also means stealing cattle but there wasn't a whole bunch of that in the backcountry as most people are honest.

sack out a process of familiarizing a horse with all the things it might have to wear or carry so it would know it was not going to be hurt. Some people started this process by rubbing a gunnysack all over a hobbled horse.

stove up stiffened up

supreme cooking test to make moose meat taste like beef

sweep a series of poles that slide along the ground and bunch up hay for transport to the stack yard, where the hay is deposited on the teeth of an overshot stocker or slide stacker to make your stack

tied one on went to bucking, running off

typical bad accident when you get bucked or dragged off a horse, kicked, shot or lost

wall tent a small structure built up about four feet high with logs and a tent on top of the highest logs

whole lot of tree about three inches

Wyoming hobble a hobble that is made from rope, instead of leather, and is about 16 feet long with a spliced eye on one end, and a spliced back on the other end

Bruce Watt sits next to Queen Elizabeth at the 1971 Williams Lake Stampede, explaining the different rodeo events. Prince Philip is on the far right. [*WILLIAMS LAKE TRIBUNE*]

ACKNOWLEDGEMENTS

Thanks to my family,

especially Kirby and Cindy,

for all their help.

Thanks also to Heidi Redl

for getting this whole thing started.

BRUCE WATT

Bruce grew up in the Fraser Valley area of BC, but it wasn't until he was in his early 20s and newly married that he moved up to the Chilcotin region of central BC. Starting out by working for Dick Church at the Big Creek Ranch on May 6, 1948, Bruce soon fell in love with this remote and wild country filled with countless interesting places, animals and people.

After a short time, the young couple purchased their own place, Breckness Ranch, and began raising their family of three girls and two boys, along with herds of cattle and horses. The work was often difficult and the conditions were rough, but it was a life they all enjoyed and the family called Big Creek home until 1973. Days were not always filled with work and Bruce certainly believed in enjoying life, so the family participated in various forms of sport.

Rodeo became a big part of Bruce's life, and he competed in the timed events of calf roping and steer wrestling, and then later took up team roping, a sport he enjoyed into his late 70s.

Bruce put in thousands of volunteer hours at the Williams Lake Stampede, judging events like the high school rodeo and the Stampede Queen contest, putting on a special rodeo for Queen Elizabeth and Prince Philip, and keeping the area grounds in immaculate condition during the Stampede. Bruce was honoured by the Canadian Professional Rodeo Association in 1994 when he was named Committee Person of the Year. He is also a member of the BC Cowboy Hall of Fame.

Always a consummate storyteller and a man of many jokes, Bruce has an uncanny ability to see the humour in most situations. He has always derived great pleasure from the people and animals around him, and Bruce's hearty laugh is second only to his thunderous sneeze.